"Leadership that Conquers Shadows: Leader or Influencer?"

Dedication

To God, a source of wisdom and constant guidance in every step of this path.

To the Ana G. Méndez University professors and administrators, for their tireless dedication and commitment to educational excellence, who have forged minds and hearts with a noble purpose.

This book is dedicated to the leaders who were, for having paved the way with their vision and courage; to the leaders who are there, for continuing to face challenges with integrity and courage; and to the leaders who will come for the future they will build with hope and determination. Your contributions inspire us all.

This book is for all of you who inspire and guide progress towards a better world.

Thanks

I want to express my deepest gratitude to my wife and children for their unconditional love, patience, and unwavering support. Your presence in my life is the most significant source of inspiration and strength. Thank you for being my refuge and believing in me every step of this journey.

To my coworkers in my business for their dedication, effort, and camaraderie. Together, we have overcome challenges and celebrated successes. Their commitment and collaboration have been essential to achieving our shared goals. Thank you for being part of this journey and making every day an opportunity for growth and learning.

INDEX

Tabla de contenido

Introduction

In the digital age, where social media and online platforms have transformed communication and influence, a crucial question arises: what differentiates an influencer from an authentic leader? While influencers capture attention and shape trends, transformational leaders are those who, beyond popularity, generate a lasting and positive impact on their followers and communities. This essay will explore this essential distinction, highlighting how authentic leadership can overcome the shadows of superficiality and short-termism, forging a path toward innovation and sustainable change.

The metaphor of "overcoming the shadows" symbolizes the ability of leaders to overcome challenges and adversities that can obscure vision and progress. Shadows can represent fear, uncertainty, resistance to change, or distractions that divert organizations and societies from their fundamental goals. A leader who overcomes these shadows provides direction and clarity and inspires others to follow their example, creating a movement towards a better future.

The term " influencer " has become popular in the modern context to describe people who can affect the decisions and behaviors of others, mainly through digital platforms. However, being an influencer does not always mean having the necessary qualities to lead effectively and sustainably. Influence can be temporary and based on image, while authentic leadership is based on integrity, vision, and the ability to motivate and transform people and organizations.

This work will examine the distinguishing characteristics of an authentic leader versus an influencer. A transformational leader has a clear vision and a defined purpose, mobilizes his team towards shared goals, and can cultivate an environment of trust and collaboration. These leaders are resilient, adaptable, and capable of making difficult decisions in times of crisis, guiding their team with empathy and firmness. In contrast, influencers can attract attention and build a following, but their impact is often limited to the surface, lacking the depth and engagement needed to lead meaningful change.

This work will illustrate how leaders who overcome the shadows address contemporary challenges through examples and case studies. Leadership strategies that emphasize innovation, sustainability, and the comprehensive development of individuals will be explored. Additionally, the importance of self-knowledge and personal leadership growth will be discussed, highlighting how these elements contribute to a leader's ability to inspire and guide others toward a promising future.

Differentiating between an influencer and an authentic leader is essential in a world where superficial influence diverts attention from what matters. By focusing on leadership that overcomes the shadows, we can cultivate leaders who inspire in the short term and build a legacy of innovation, resilience, and sustainable progress. The book will provide a comprehensive guide for those who aspire to lead with integrity and purpose, overcoming the shadows of superficiality and forging a path to a better future.

Chapter 1: Influencer vs Leader

In the contemporary world, where social networks and digital communication dominate, it is crucial to distinguish between the concepts of influencer and leader. At first glance, both may seem similar due to their ability to attract and mobilize many followers. However, deeper exploration reveals essential differences that define their influence and impact on society.

Differences and Similarities between an Influencer and a Leader.

Purpose and Motivation.

Purpose and motivation are the first fundamental differences between an influencer and a leader. Influencers often seek visibility and popularity. Their main objective is to attract and maintain a broad audience, monetizing their presence through sponsorships, advertising, and collaborations. Likes, followers, and shares measure an influencer's influence. For example, Kim Kardashian, one of the best-known influencers, has built an empire based on her presence on social networks, influencing fashion, beauty, and lifestyle.

In contrast, a leader is motivated by a long-term vision and purpose. Its objective is to guide, inspire, and transform its followers, promoting personal and organizational development. A leader's influence is based on integrity, vision, and the ability to motivate others to achieve shared goals. Mahatma Gandhi, for example, did not seek popularity; his leadership was driven by a deep conviction of justice and freedom, leading millions towards Indian independence through non-violence.

Depth of Influence.

Influencers' influence tends to be superficial and focused on specific aspects such as fashion, lifestyle, or product consumption. This connection with the audience can be temporary and based on passing trends. An influencer can shape opinions and behaviors in the short term but rarely induces significant and sustainable changes.

On the other hand, a leader's influence is profound and lasting. Transformational leaders create a significant impact that encompasses cultural, organizational, and social change. Nelson Mandela, for example, not only led the fight against apartheid in South Africa; his leadership transformed the nation, fostering reconciliation and racial equality. Authentic leaders leave a legacy that lasts beyond their time.

Mechanisms of Influence.

Influencers primarily use digital platforms and media to reach and persuade their audience. Their power of influence is measured by their ability to generate immediate reactions on social networks. For example, PewDiePie (Felix Kjellberg), a prominent YouTube influencer, has significantly impacted digital culture through his entertainment content.

In contrast, leaders use a combination of effective communication, personal examples, and organizational strategies to guide and motivate their followers. Positive and sustainable changes within an organization or community measure its influence. Jacinda Ardern, Prime Minister of New Zealand, has demonstrated empathetic and effective leadership, especially during the COVID-19 crisis, guiding her nation with clarity and compassion.

Responsability and compromise.

An influencer's responsibility is usually to improve their public image and perception of the audience. Their commitment may be limited to specific campaigns and collaborations. The relationship between the influencer and their audience is often transactional, based on exchanging content for attention.

On the other hand, a leader has a profound responsibility towards the well-being and development of his followers. A leader's continuous commitment encompasses all aspects of organizational and community life. Satya Nadella, CEO of Microsoft, has led a significant transformation in the company's culture, promoting innovation and inclusive growth and demonstrating a long-term commitment to the organization's vision and values.

Historical and Contemporary Examples of Influencers and Leaders.

Historical and Contemporary Influencers.

In the 19th century, Lydia Pinkham used her image and reputation to promote her medicinal tonics, becoming one of the first influencers in health and wellness. In contemporary times, figures such as Kim Kardashian and PewDiePie have capitalized on their presence on social networks to influence millions of people, shaping trends and behaviors in various areas.

Historical and Contemporary Leaders.

Mahatma Gandhi and Nelson Mandela are classic examples of transformational leaders whose legacies have left an indelible mark on history. Today, leaders like Jacinda Ardern and Satya Nadella continue to demonstrate how authentic leadership can overcome the shadows and guide their followers toward a promising future.

In short, while influencers and leaders may share certain similarities regarding visibility and communication skills, their motivations, depth of influence, and responsibilities differ significantly. Understanding these differences is crucial to recognizing and fostering leadership that guides, motivates, transforms, and overcomes the shadows of the present. By focusing on authentic leadership, we can cultivate leaders who inspire lasting, positive change, building a brighter, more sustainable future.

Chapter 2: History of Leadership

The concept of leadership has evolved significantly throughout history, adapting to social, political, and economic changes. From the first civilizations to the modern world, leadership has been essential for the organization and progress of societies. Below is a tour of the different stages of this evolution.

In ancient civilizations, leadership was often associated with divine power and absolute authority. Egyptian pharaohs, for example, were considered gods on Earth, and their leadership was based on theocracy and divine command. In Mesopotamia, kings were also seen as representatives of the gods, and their leadership focused on administering laws and constructing infrastructure.

Ancient Greece, particularly in Athens, introduced a more democratic form of leadership. Leaders were elected by the people and expected to act in their best interests. This democratic evolution was further enriched by the philosophical explorations of Plato and Aristotle, who delved into the qualities and virtues necessary for a good leader. In Rome, leadership took on a new form, blending military and administrative skills, with charismatic and strategically adept figures like Julius Caesar and Augustus at the helm.

During the Middle Ages, leadership was dominated by the monarch, whose authority was based on the divine right of kings. Feudal lords also exercised significant local leadership based on loyalty and vassalage. The Catholic Church played a crucial role in legitimizing leadership, with the Pope and bishops wielding considerable power in spiritual and temporal matters.

The Age of Discovery brought with it an expansion of global leadership, with European explorers and conquerors leading expeditions and establishing colonies. For its part, the Enlightenment questioned the traditional bases of leadership, promoting ideas of rationality, equality, and individual rights. Philosophers such as John Locke and Montesquieu influenced the modern conception of political leadership, which moved away from absolutism towards more democratic and participatory models.

The Industrial Revolution transformed business leadership, highlighting the importance of efficiency, organization, and innovation. Industrial leaders such as Henry Ford and Andrew Carnegie exemplified leadership in the era of mass production. In the 20th century, military and political leadership came to the fore during the world wars, with figures such as Winston Churchill and Franklin D. Roosevelt demonstrating how leadership can be crucial in times of crisis.

Today, leadership is more complex and multifaceted, influenced by globalization, technology, and social changes. Transformational leadership, focused on inspiration and empowerment, has become a prevalent model. Additionally, inclusive and diverse leadership is recognized, which values different perspectives and fosters a collaborative and equitable environment.

Main Leadership Theories.

Several leadership theories have emerged throughout history to explain how and why certain people become effective leaders. Below are some of the most influential theories.

Theory of the Great Man.

One of the earliest leadership theories, the Great Man theory, argues that leaders are born with innate qualities that distinguish them from others. This theory is based on the belief that certain people are destined to lead due to their exceptional characteristics. Historical examples include figures such as Alexander the Great and Napoleon Bonaparte.

Trait Theory.

Trait theory suggests that leaders possess certain personal traits that make them effective. These traits may include intelligence, self-confidence, determination, and sociability. This theory has identified key competencies and skills that can predict leadership potential.

Behavioral Theory.

Unlike trait theories, behavioral theory focuses on leaders' actions and behaviors. This theory distinguishes between leadership styles, such as authoritarian, democratic, and laissez-faire, and examines how these styles affect leadership effectiveness.

Contingency Theory.

Contingency theory maintains that no single leadership style is effective in all situations. Instead, leadership effectiveness depends on the fit between the leader's style and the specific demands of the problem. Notable examples of this theory include Fiedler's contingency model and path-goal theory.

Transformational Leadership Theory.

Developed by James MacGregor Burns and Bernard Bass, transformational leadership theory focuses on leaders' ability to inspire and motivate their followers. Transformational leaders are seen as change agents who foster high commitment and performance in their followers, promoting a shared vision and personal and professional growth.

Transactional Leadership Theory.

Contrasted with the theory of transformational leadership, transactional leadership is based on the exchange of rewards and punishments to influence followers' behavior. Transactional leaders set clear goals and use incentives to motivate their followers to meet them.

Situational Leadership Theory.

Situational leadership theory, developed by Paul Hersey and Ken Blanchard, suggests that leaders should adapt their leadership style based on the maturity and competence of their followers. This theory identifies four main leadership styles: directive, persuasive, participative, and delegation.

The evolution of leadership over the centuries and the development of various leadership theories offer us a richer and more nuanced understanding of what it means to be an effective leader. From the ancient pharaohs to the transformational leaders of the 21st century, leadership has been and will continue to be a crucial force for human progress. By studying the different theories and models, we can better equip ourselves to meet leadership challenges in the contemporary world, fostering leadership that guides, inspires, and transforms.

Chapter 3: History of Influencers

The rise of influencers is inextricably linked to the advent of the digital age and the proliferation of social media. Over the past two decades, digital platforms have transformed how people communicate, consume content, and make decisions. This change has given rise to a new type of public figure: the influencer.

The First Digital Influencers.

The concept of influencers is not new; public figures and celebrities have influenced public opinion and trends for centuries. However, the digital age has democratized this influence, allowing individuals to achieve mass visibility without needing a traditional platform. The first digital influencers emerged in the mid-2000s, popularizing blogs and platforms like YouTube and MySpace. These pioneers took advantage of direct access to a global audience to share and quickly gained knowledge and talents.

One of the first examples of digital influencers is PewDiePie (Felix Kjellberg), who began posting gaming videos to YouTube in 2010. Over time, his channel became one of the most subscribed to on the platform, demonstrating the power of digital influence. Another early example is Perez Hilton, who started his celebrity gossip blog in 2004 and quickly gained notoriety and followers.

With the growth of social media platforms such as Facebook, Twitter, Instagram, and Snapchat, people's ability to become influencers has expanded exponentially.

Each platform offered new ways to connect with audiences and different content formats. Instagram, launched in 2010, quickly became a hotbed for fashion, beauty, fitness, and lifestyle influencers due to its focus on visual content.

As platforms evolved, so did the types of influencers. They diversified into specific niches, including beauty, fashion, fitness, travel, food, technology, etc. This diversification allowed influencers to build highly engaged and segmented audiences, increasing their appeal to brands and advertisers.

Social networks have been the primary catalyst for the creation and expansion of the influencer phenomenon. These platforms have provided the perfect medium for individuals to share content, connect with their audiences, and monetize their influence.

Key Platforms and Their Influence.

Youtube:

Video Content: YouTube allows content creators to share videos on various topics, from makeup tutorials to product reviews to daily vlogs. The platform incentivized creators with the ad monetization program, allowing many influencers to earn significant income.

Example: Bethany Mota, one of the first and most successful beauty influencers on YouTube, used the platform to share fashion and makeup tips, amassing millions of followers.

Instagram:

Visual Content: Instagram, with its focus on photos and short videos, has become the ideal platform for fashion, beauty, and lifestyle influencers. Features like Stories and IGTV expanded the opportunities for content creation.

Example: Chiara Ferragni, a fashion influencer who started her blog in 2009, took advantage of Instagram to share her style and daily life, becoming one of the most followed influencers in the world.

Twitter:

Microblogging: Twitter allows influencers to share thoughts, news, and links in real-time. Although less visual than other platforms, it has been crucial for influencers in politics, technology, and business.

Example: Elon Musk, CEO of Tesla and SpaceX, uses Twitter to communicate directly with his followers, influence markets, and give his opinion on various topics.

TikTok:

Short and Creative Videos: TikTok revolutionized short video content, allowing users to create and share 15- to 60-second clips with music, effects, and filters. The platform has given rise to a new generation of young influencers.

Example: Charli D'Amelio, who became one of TikTok's top stars with her dance videos, amassing millions of followers quickly.

Monetization and Collaborations with Brands.

Influencer creation is also reflected in the monetization opportunities they offer. Brands have recognized the power of influencers to reach specific audiences and have invested in collaborations, sponsorships, and affiliate marketing. Influencers can earn income through various sources, including:

Paid Sponsorships: Direct collaborations with brands to promote products or services.

Platform Advertising: Income generated through monetization programs like YouTube or Instagram ads.

Affiliate Marketing: Commissions on sales generated through affiliate links shared by influencers.

Products and Merchandising: Sale of own products, from clothing lines to books and online courses.

The rise of influencers in the digital age has redefined the concept of influence and leadership. Social media has allowed ordinary individuals to achieve massive visibility and build lucrative careers by sharing their passions and knowledge. As digital platforms evolve, the influencer phenomenon will continue to adapt, offering new opportunities and challenges for content creators and brands.

Chapter 4: Characteristics of an Effective Leader

Common Traits in Successful Leaders.

Influential leaders possess a unique combination of personal traits and skills that enable them to guide, inspire, and motivate their followers toward achieving common goals.

Influential leaders have a clear vision of the future and a defined purpose that guides their actions. This vision provides direction and motivation for both the leader and his followers. A leader with a strong vision can inspire others to work toward long-term goals, overcoming obstacles and challenges.

Integrity is an essential trait for any leader. It involves being honest, ethical, and consistent in actions and decisions. Leaders who act with integrity earn the trust and respect of their followers, creating an environment of transparency and trust.

The ability to communicate clearly and persuasively is crucial to leadership. Influential leaders are good listeners and know how to convey their ideas in a way that everyone can understand and support. Communication involves speaking, actively listening, and responding appropriately to followers' concerns.

Empathy is a powerful tool in a leader's arsenal. It enables them to understand and connect with the emotions and needs of their followers. An empathetic leader fosters an environment of support and understanding, which, in turn, cultivates team members' loyalty and commitment.

Resilience, a defining characteristic of influential leaders, enables them to bounce back from adversity and maintain emotional stability in times of crisis. It ensures that leaders stay focused on their objectives, adapting to changing circumstances with flexibility and determination.

Making informed and timely decisions is a critical leadership skill. Influential leaders evaluate complex situations, consider multiple perspectives, and make decisions that benefit the group. Confidence in decision-making also helps followers feel safe and directed.

Influential leaders inspire and motivate their followers to reach their full potential. They use various techniques, such as recognition, rewards, or simply being a role model, to foster enthusiasm and commitment.

In an ever-changing world, adaptability is an essential trait for leadership. Influential leaders can adjust their strategies and approaches to meet new challenges and seize new opportunities.

How to Develop Leadership Skills.

Developing leadership skills is an ongoing process that requires dedication and practice.

Participating in leadership training and education programs can provide valuable knowledge and practical tools. Leadership courses, workshops, and seminars offer learning opportunities from experts and the opportunity to share experiences with other leaders.

Seeking guidance from mentors and leadership coaches can accelerate skill development. Mentors can provide advice based on experience, while coaches can offer personalized feedback and support to improve leadership skills.

Practice is essential to developing leadership skills. Taking on leadership roles in projects, teams, or communities allows individuals to apply what they have learned and gain real experience. Practice also helps identify areas for improvement and personal strengths.

Regular reflection on one's experiences and behaviors is crucial for leadership development. Keeping a leadership journal, for example, can help individuals identify patterns, recognize successes, and learn from mistakes.

Improving communication skills is essential for any leader. Active listening, public speaking, and persuasive writing can strengthen leaders' ability to convey their vision and connect with their followers.

Developing empathy involves practicing active listening and showing a genuine interest in the experiences and feelings of others. Engaging in activities that promote mutual understanding and support can increase empathy in leadership.

Setting clear goals and evaluating progress regularly can help leaders stay focused and motivated. Goals should be specific, measurable, attainable, relevant, and time-bound (SMART).

Feedback from colleagues, mentors, and followers is essential for leadership growth. Constructive feedback provides valuable information about strengths and areas for improvement and helps leaders adjust their approach and behavior.

Influential leaders possess a combination of personal traits and skills that allow them to guide and inspire their followers toward achieving common goals. Although some characteristics may be innate, many leadership skills can be developed and strengthened through education, experience, and reflection. By focusing on continuous development and personal improvement, any individual can cultivate the qualities necessary to become an effective leader who overcomes the shadows and guides his team toward a promising future.

Chapter 5: Characteristics of an Effective Influencer

Influencers Use.

Influencers share certain traits and employ strategies to attract and maintain their audiences. Below are some of the most common characteristics and tactics among successful influencers.

One of the most essential traits of an effective influencer is authenticity. Followers are more likely to connect with and trust someone genuine and transparent. Authenticity involves sharing real experiences, emotions, and honest opinions, which helps build a stronger, longer-lasting relationship with your audience.

Successful influencers are usually passionate and knowledgeable about the topics they cover. This passion and knowledge make them more credible and allow them to create valuable and relevant content for their audience. Whether in fashion, technology, fitness, or any other niche, experience and enthusiasm are essential.

Consistency in posting content is crucial to maintaining follower interest and engagement. Influential influencers have a regular posting schedule and stick to it, consistently providing fresh and relevant content. This consistency helps maintain visibility and relevance on social media platforms.

An influencer's ability to communicate clearly and attractively is essential. This includes the ability to speak and write well and the ability to tell stories in ways that resonate with the audience. Storytelling is a powerful tool that helps influencers connect emotionally with their followers.

Successful influencers actively interact with their audience. They respond to comments and direct messages and participate in online conversations. This interaction strengthens the relationship with followers and provides valuable feedback that can help improve content and strategy.

Collaborations with other brands and influencers can expand an influencer's reach and influence. To be effective, these partnerships must be strategic and aligned with the influencer's values and style. Successful collaborations can attract new followers and provide new content opportunities.

Creativity is critical to standing out in a saturated market. Influential influencers find unique ways to present content and engage their audience. This can include using different content formats, such as videos, photos, and infographics, and experimenting with new trends and platforms.

The world of social media is constantly changing, and influential influencers can quickly adapt to new trends, platforms, and algorithms. The ability to change and evolve with the digital environment is crucial to maintaining long-term relevance and success.

The Importance of Authenticity in Social Networks.

Authenticity is one of the fundamental pillars for success on social networks. Being authentic can set an influencer apart in an environment where competition for attention is fierce. Below are some reasons why authenticity is so important.

Authenticity helps build trust with the audience. Followers are more likely to trust someone honest and genuine. This trust is essential to maintaining a robust and long-lasting relationship with followers, which is crucial for long-term success.

Being authentic allows influencers to connect emotionally with their audience. Sharing personal experiences, successes, and failures helps followers see the influencer as natural and relatable. This emotional connection can strengthen the bond between the influencer and their audience.

Authenticity can be a differentiating factor in a market saturated with content and competition. Followers can detect a lack of authenticity and are more likely to gravitate toward influencers who come across as genuine and transparent. Authenticity can help an influencer stand out and attract a loyal audience.

Authenticity is sustainable in the long term. Faking a personality or lifestyle can be exhausting and challenging to maintain. Authentic influencers can keep their focus and content over time without the stress of maintaining a facade.

Loyal followers are those who not only follow the influencer for their content but also actively support and promote them. Authenticity helps attract and retain these loyal followers, who are more likely to engage, share, and advocate for the influencer.

Authenticity can improve an influencer's reputation. A good reputation attracts more followers and collaboration opportunities with brands and other influencers. Authenticity creates a positive and trustworthy image, which is crucial for success on social media.

Influencers share several traits and strategies that allow them to attract and maintain their audience. Authenticity, consistency, creativity, and active interaction with followers are some key characteristics that contribute to an influencer's success. In a saturated digital world, authenticity helps differentiate yourself and builds the trust and loyalty necessary for lasting impact. By focusing on these traits and strategies, influencers can create a robust and sustainable social media presence.

Chapter 6: Influence vs. Leadership

How Influence and Leadership Intertwine.

Influence and leadership are closely related concepts that overlap in the modern context. Although they have fundamental differences, both are crucial in guiding and motivating others.

Influence: Influence refers to the ability to affect the decisions, actions, and opinions of others. It is based on persuasion and the ability to attract attention and interest. Influencers use their presence and charisma to guide the trends and behaviors of their audience.

Leadership: Leadership involves guiding and directing a group toward achieving common goals. A leader not only influences but also inspires, motivates, and organizes. Effective leadership is based on vision, integrity, and the ability to foster collaboration and long-term commitment.

Influence is an essential tool of leadership. An effective leader must be able to influence his followers to adopt the group's vision and goals. This includes persuading, motivating, and guiding people to work together towards a common goal. In this sense, influence is a fundamental component of leadership.

Reach: Influence can have a broad and rapid reach, especially in the digital context. A single post by an influencer can reach millions of people. However, this influence can be superficial and short-term.

Depth: Leadership, on the other hand, seeks more profound, lasting influence. A leader wants to change people's opinions, behavior, and commitment long-term. This requires a stronger connection and investment in follower development.

Trust and credibility are essential for both influence and leadership. However, the way they are constructed may differ. Influencers often gain credibility through authenticity and consistency in their messages. In addition to these factors, leaders must demonstrate integrity, competence, and a genuine commitment to the well-being of their followers.

Influencer's liability is often limited to the quality and integrity of the content they share. Your engagement can be transactional and based on specific campaigns.

Leaders have a broader responsibility that includes the well-being and development of their followers. Their continuous commitment focuses on achieving long-term objectives and maintaining a positive and productive environment.

Some figures in today's world have successfully combined influence and leadership, using their platform to inspire and guide others meaningfully. Below are some notable examples.

Elon Musk, CEO of Tesla and SpaceX, is a clear example of a figure who is both an influencer and a leader. Musk uses platforms like Twitter to communicate directly with the public, influence markets, and share his vision for the future. His ability to inspire through his vision and leadership in technology and sustainability has gained a massive following. Additionally, its influence extends beyond social media, significantly impacting the automotive and aerospace industries.

Oprah Winfrey is another iconic figure who has combined influence and leadership. Oprah has influenced millions of people through her television show, magazines, and digital platforms. However, her impact goes beyond media influence. Oprah has demonstrated effective leadership by empowering people, promoting education and wellness, and leading significant philanthropic initiatives. His leadership is based on authenticity, empathy, and a vision of a better world.

Malala Yousafzai, a girls' education activist and the youngest winner of the Nobel Peace Prize, has used her influence to advocate for girls' rights to education worldwide. Through her speeches, books, and social media presence, Malala has inspired millions of people. Her leadership manifests in her courage, commitment to justice, and ability to mobilize others around a vital cause.

Influence and leadership are interconnected concepts that, when combined, can create significant and lasting impact. While influence can capture attention and motivate in the short term, leadership focuses on guiding and sustaining that impact through vision, integrity, and commitment. Figures such as Elon Musk, Oprah Winfrey, Malala Yousafzai, and Greta Thunberg demonstrate how the combination of influence and leadership can inspire and transform communities and the world. By understanding how these concepts intertwine, we can aspire to be leaders who influence, guide, and motivate toward a better future.

Chapter 7: Alexander Otaola: Influence and Leadership

Alexander Otaola is a Cuban American public figure who has effectively combined the roles of influencer and leader within the Cuban exile community. Known primarily for his "Hola Ota -Ola" program on YouTube, Otaola addresses political, social, and cultural issues related to Cuba and the Cuban diaspora. His ability to influence public opinion and mobilize people around common causes makes him an interesting case study of how influence and leadership are intertwined.

Influence of Alexander Otaola.

Alexander Otaola has built a large audience on digital platforms such as YouTube, Facebook, and Instagram. Its content is often controversial and polarizing, which has allowed it to capture the attention and maintain the interest of a broad audience.

Authenticity and Passion: Otaola is distinguished by its authentic and passionate style. He is not afraid to express his opinions directly and forcefully, which has resonated with many followers who seek a frank and uncensored voice in the debate about Cuba.

Consistency: You post content regularly, keeping your audience engaged and up-to-date on current events and your interpretation of these events. This consistency has been crucial to his success as an influencer.

Interaction with Audience: Otaola actively interacts with its followers through comments, live sessions, and social networks. This interaction strengthens your relationship with your audience and allows you to capture and respond to your community's concerns and opinions.

Controversy and Provocation: Otaola often uses controversy to gain attention. His willingness to address sensitive topics and provocative style have allowed him to stand out in the crowded social media.

Storytelling: You are a compelling storyteller who uses personal stories and anecdotes to connect emotionally with your audience. This technique allows you to humanize your topics and make them more accessible to your audience.

Visuals and Production: Otaola pays close attention to the production quality of its content, using graphics, video clips, and other visual elements to keep its audience engaged.

The leadership of Alexander Otaola.

Alexander Otaola not only seeks to entertain; Their work has a clear purpose and long-term vision. It aspires to promote political change in Cuba and raise awareness about the realities that Cubans face both on the island and in exile.

Clear Vision: His vision of political and social change in Cuba is always present in its content. This consistent and consistent approach allows you to inspire others to share and support your cause.

Defined Purpose: Otaola uses its platform to inform, mobilize, and empower the Cuban community in exile. This purpose gives you a clear direction and motivates your followers to participate actively.

Mobilization and Organization.

Protests and Events: You have organized and participated in numerous demonstrations and community events. Your ability to mobilize people around specific causes demonstrates your leadership effectiveness.

Political Campaigns: Otaola has been instrumental in promoting political and awareness campaigns, using its platform to amplify essential messages and calls to action.

Inspiration and Motivation.

Community Empowerment: Through her content, Otaola empowers her followers to be more politically active and use their voices to demand change. Your ability to inspire action reflects genuine leadership.

Behavior Modeling: Acts as a role model, showing how media influence can be used for constructive, high-impact purposes. Their example encourages others to take a more active role in fighting for their rights and freedoms.

Credibility and Trust.

Transparency: Transparency in his opinions and actions has allowed him to gain the trust of his audience. Otaola's followers value his honesty and the perception that he is not afraid to tell the truth, regardless of the consequences.

Integrity: Despite controversies, he has maintained a firm and consistent stance, cemented his reputation as an authentic and trusted voice within the Cuban community.

Concrete Examples of Influence and Leadership.

One of Otaola's most notable campaigns was organizing and promoting protests in Miami to support protesters in Cuba during the July 11, 2021, demonstrations. He used his platform to mobilize thousands of people, providing updates in real-time and strategies to maximize the impact of protests.

Otaola has collaborated with other community leaders and public figures to amplify his message and reach a broader audience. These collaborations have included interviews with politicians, activists, and other influencers, strengthening his position as an opinion leader.

Alexander Otaola exemplifies how influence and leadership can be combined to create a significant impact. His ability to attract and maintain a large and engaged audience, his clear vision, and his ability to mobilize the community make him a unique figure in digital media and activism. By understanding and applying the lessons of his approach, others can learn to be effective influencers and leaders who guide their communities toward a better future.

Chapter 8: Ethics in Leadership

Ethical leadership is based on principles that guide leaders in their decision-making and daily behavior. These principles are fundamental to establishing and maintaining trust, credibility, and respect within an organization or community.

Integrity involves honesty and strong moral principles. Leaders of integrity are consistent in their actions, decisions, and words, which allows them to gain and maintain the trust of their followers. Integrity also means admitting mistakes and being transparent in communication.

Justice is fundamental in ethical leadership. Leaders must treat all their followers equally and without favoritism. This includes making decisions based on objective and fair criteria and ensuring everyone has the same opportunities.

Ethical leaders take responsibility for their actions and decisions. This means they accept the consequences of their choices and do not blame others for their mistakes. Responsibility also means being proactive in problem-solving and continuous improvement.

Respect for others is essential in ethical leadership. Leaders must value the contributions and opinions of their followers, regardless of their differences. Fostering an environment of mutual respect and consideration helps build a positive and collaborative organizational culture.

Transparency is critical to establishing trust and credibility. Leaders must be open and sincere in their communication, providing the information necessary for their followers to understand their decisions and actions.

Empathy allows leaders to understand and connect with their followers' emotions and needs. This improves the leader—followers' relationships and helps them make more informed and compassionate decisions.

Ethical leadership involves a focus on service to others. Leaders must prioritize the well-being of their followers and the community above their interests. This servant leadership approach fosters a culture of support and collaboration.

Nelson Mandela, South Africa's first black president, is an emblematic example of ethical leadership. During his life, he fought against apartheid and worked tirelessly for justice and reconciliation in his country.

Mandela maintained his principles and values even during the 27 years he spent in prison. He never compromised his integrity despite adversity. He worked to dismantle the apartheid system and establish a just and equal society in South Africa. It promoted reconciliation and mutual respect between different races and communities, avoiding revenge and encouraging unity. He showed deep empathy towards all the people of South Africa, understanding the suffering of the black population and also reaching out to those who had been their oppressors, promoting forgiveness and reconciliation. Mandela dedicated his life to serving his country and its people, prioritizing collective well-being over his well-being.

Nelson Mandela is remembered as a political leader and a global symbol of integrity, justice, and reconciliation. His legacy continues to inspire leaders around the world.

Kenneth Lay, founder and CEO of Enron, is an example of unethical leadership. Enron was one of the largest energy companies in the world before collapsing in 2001 due to one of the largest accounting scandals in US history.

Lay and other Enron executives misled investors and employees about the company's financial condition. They manipulated financial statements to show false profits and hide debts. Enron's practices seriously harmed employees, investors, and the economy as a whole. Thousands of employees lost their jobs and life savings. Lay and other executives did not take responsibility for their actions. Instead, they tried to blame others and minimized their involvement in the fraud. Lack of transparency was a hallmark of the Enron scandal. Executives withheld crucial information from investors, regulators, and employees.

The collapse of Enron had devastating consequences for its employees, investors, and the financial market in general. The scandal led to the enactment of the Sarbanes-Oxley Act in 2002, which was intended to improve company transparency and accountability.

Ethics in leadership is essential to building and maintaining trust, credibility, and respect within an organization or community. Ethical principles, such as integrity, fairness, responsibility, respect, transparency, empathy, and service, are essential for effective and sustainable leadership. The cases of Nelson Mandela and Kenneth Lay illustrate the consequences of adhering to or violating these ethical principles. While ethical leadership can inspire and transform societies, unethical leadership can cause irreparable harm. Therefore, leaders must aspire to maintain high ethical standards in all their actions and decisions.

Chapter 9: Ethics in Influencer Marketing

The Importance of Transparency and Authenticity.

In influencer marketing, transparency and authenticity are fundamental pillars determining the credibility and trust that followers place in influencers.

Transparency in influencer marketing means that influencers must be transparent and honest about their business relationships. This includes disclosing any payments or compensation for promoting a product or service. Transparency is crucial for several reasons:

Trust: Trust is the foundation of any relationship, especially that between influencers and their followers. Lack of transparency can erode this trust and damage the influencer's reputation.

Legality: Many countries have regulations requiring disclosure of paid relationships. For example, the Federal Trade Commission (FTC) requires influencers to disclose any material relationships with brands in the United States.

Ethics: Being transparent about business relationships is an ethical practice that demonstrates integrity and respect towards the audience.

Authenticity refers to the genuineness with which an influencer presents their opinions and recommendations. Followers value authenticity because it allows them to believe that the influencer's opinions are honest and not simply motivated by money. Authenticity in influencer marketing is essential for the following reasons:

Credibility: Authentic influencers are perceived as more credible and trustworthy. This can increase the effectiveness of your recommendations and your followers' loyalty.

Engagement: Authenticity encourages greater engagement, as followers feel connected with a natural person, not a manufactured figure.

Sustainability: Authenticity is sustainable in the long term. Authentic influencers can maintain their voice and style without compromising their personal values.

To illustrate the importance of transparency and authenticity in influencer marketing, below are cases of ethical and unethical practices.

Case 1: Ethical Practices - Diipa Khosla.

Diipa Khosla, a fashion and beauty influencer, is known for the transparency and authenticity of her brand relationships. Khosla always discloses his collaborations and sponsorships clearly and openly.

Clear Disclosure: Diipa Khosla uses tags like #ad or #sponsored on his sponsored posts to indicate when a post is a paid collaboration.

Genuine Reviews: Although he works with brands, Khosla tests and approves products before recommending them to his followers. You only promote products you like and believe bring value to your audience.

Transparency in the Process: Share with your followers how you select the brands you collaborate with, explaining your criteria and selection processes. This transparency increases the trust and respect of your audience.

Diipa 's ethical practices in Khosla have strengthened their credibility and the loyalty of their audience. His transparent and authentic approach has made his recommendations highly valued and influential.

Case 2: Unethical Practices - Fyre Festival Influencers.

The Fyre Festival billed as a luxury music event on a private island, became a monumental fiasco. Several high-profile influencers, including Kendall Jenner and Bella Hadid, promoted the festival without disclosing their compensation.

Lack of Disclosure: Many influencers who promoted the Fyre Festival did not disclose that they had received payments for their posts. This violated the FTC's guidelines on disclosure of business relationships.

Misleading Promotion: Influencers promoted the festival as a luxury experience without verifying the authenticity of the event's promises. The misleading promotion contributed to the perception that the event would be much more than it was.

Negative Consequences: The lack of transparency and misleading promotion resulted in a significant loss of trust among followers and damage to the influencers' reputations.

The Fyre Festival scandal highlighted the importance of transparency and authenticity in influencer marketing. The influencers involved faced severe criticism and some legal action, underscoring the need for ethical practices in their business relationships.

Transparency and authenticity are crucial elements in influencer marketing. A lack of these can lead to losing trust, credibility, and possible legal repercussions. On the other hand, adherence to these ethical principles can strengthen the relationship between the influencer and their audience, increase the effectiveness of marketing campaigns, and ensure long-term sustainability. The Diipa cases of Khosla and the Fyre Festival illustrate the consequences of ethical and unethical practices. By prioritizing transparency and authenticity, influencers can maintain the integrity of their brand and promote more honest and effective marketing.

Chapter 10: Interview with Amanda, a Crystal Generation Influencer

Author: Good afternoon, Amanda. Thank you for taking the time to talk to me today about ethics and principles in influencer marketing. Please tell us a little about yourself and how you became an influencer.

Amanda: Sure, it's a pleasure to be here. I'm Amanda, 25 years old, and I started sharing my life and passions on social media about two years ago. It began as a hobby, sharing fashion, beauty, and lifestyle tips. My audience grew gradually, and I started collaborating with brands. Today, I strive to be an authentic and responsible voice for my followers, especially those of my generation.

Author: That sounds great, Amanda. Ethics in influencer marketing is an important topic today. What ethical principles do you consider fundamental in your work?

Amanda: Transparency and authenticity are essential for me. I always make it clear when a post is sponsored and make sure my followers know my opinions are genuine. Additionally, promoting products and brands I genuinely believe in and use personally is necessary. I don't want to sell something just for the money; I want my followers to trust me and know I will always be honest.

Author: You mentioned transparency as a critical principle. Could you give us an example of how you implement it in your daily life as an influencer?

Amanda: Of course. I always use tags like #ad or #sponsored in my paid posts. Additionally, I often openly discuss my relationship with the brands I collaborate with. For example, if I'm promoting a product, I explain how I use it, why I like it, and how it can benefit my followers. I also try products before recommending them to give an honest and informed opinion.

Author: That's excellent. Authenticity is another key point you mentioned. How do you maintain authenticity in an environment where influencers are often expected to project a perfect image?

Amanda: It's a challenge, for sure. It's important to show not only the positive aspects of my life but also the challenges and imperfections. Sharing my struggles and being honest about difficult days helps me connect more realistically with my followers. Perfection is unrealistic, and I want my followers to know it's okay not to be perfect. Being vulnerable and authentic allows me to build a stronger and more loyal community.

Author: That is very inspiring. Speaking of challenges, what are some of the most significant ethical dilemmas you face as an influencer, and how do you handle them?

Amanda: One of the biggest dilemmas is deciding which brands to collaborate with. I received many offers, but not all aligned with my values or what I want to represent. I take the time to research each brand and understand their practices before agreeing to a collaboration. Another challenge is the pressure always to be active and relevant, which can lead to the temptation to post content that is not genuine. To manage this, I take regular breaks from social media and prioritize my mental well-being.

Author: It's admirable that you prioritize integrity and authenticity in your work. What advice would you give to other young influencers who are starting and want to stay true to their ethical principles?

Amanda: My advice is always to be true to yourself and your values. Don't compromise your integrity for fame or money. Building a loyal and authentic audience may take time, but it is much more rewarding and sustainable in the long term. Educating yourself on regulations and best practices in influencer marketing is also essential to meet ethical and legal standards.

Author: Thank you, Amanda. It has been very enriching to hear your perspectives. Do you have any final message for your followers and for those who admire you for your ethics and authenticity?

Amanda: I want to thank all my followers for their continued support. My final message would be to remain authentic to yourself, regardless of external pressures. Authenticity and integrity are the foundation of any lasting success. And remember, it's okay to be imperfect and vulnerable. That is what makes us human and truly connects us to others.

Author: Thanks again, Amanda. It has been a pleasure speaking with you and learning from your ethical approach to influencer marketing. I am sure your words will inspire many.

Amanda: Thank you. It has been an honor to share my thoughts, and I hope we can continue to promote transparency and authenticity in this field.

This interview with Amanda, an influencer from Cristal's generation, highlights the importance of ethics, transparency, and authenticity in influencer marketing. Their experiences and advice provide valuable insight into how influencers can maintain high ethical standards while building and maintaining a trusting relationship with their followers.

Amanda Camaraza (@caamy_98)

Chapter 11: Impact of Leadership on Society

Leaders shape and change society. Leadership has a profound and lasting impact on society. Leaders can influence how a community, an organization, or even a nation develops through their vision, actions, and decisions. This impact can manifest itself in several ways:

Leaders can inspire and motivate people to reach their full potential. Through their vision and charisma, they can mobilize individuals and groups toward common goals, fostering a sense of purpose and direction. This improves individual and collective performance and can lead to positive cultural change.

Leaders are often the drivers of innovation and progress. Your ability to identify opportunities, challenge, and foster creativity can lead to significant advances in diverse areas, from technology and science to politics and art. Innovative leaders foster an environment where creative thinking is valued and rewarded.

Leaders also play a crucial role in promoting justice and equity in society. Through policies and actions that address inequalities and foster inclusion, leaders can help create more just and equitable societies. This includes defending human rights and social justice and fighting against discrimination.

Effective leadership can be a determining factor in stabilizing and resolving crises or conflicts. Leaders who manage difficult situations calmly, clearly, and compassionately can guide their communities toward conflict resolution and reconstruction. Their ability to mediate and negotiate can prevent tensions from escalating and promote reconciliation.

Leadership is also essential for sustainable development. Leaders who prioritize sustainability can influence policies and practices that protect the environment and ensure the well-being of future generations. This includes promoting renewable energy, conserving natural resources, and encouraging responsible business practices. To illustrate how leaders can shape and change society, below are examples of leaders who have significantly impacted their communities and beyond.

Wangari Maathai.

An environmental activist and Kenyan politician, she founded the Green Belt Movement, an organization focused on environmental conservation and improving women's livelihoods through tree planting. Maathai promoted reforestation in Kenya and Africa by planting more than 30 million trees. Their efforts helped combat deforestation, soil erosion, and climate change. Through her work, Maathai empowered thousands of rural women, providing them employment and improving their quality of life. His transformational leadership combined environmental and social justice.

Aung San Suu Kyi.

Burmese political leader and activist, she was a crucial figure in the fight for democracy in Myanmar.

Despite controversies and challenges, his influence on Burmese politics has been significant. Suu Kyi spent years under house arrest due to his opposition to Myanmar's military regime. His dedication to the cause of democracy inspired many and brought international attention to the situation in his country. Although his leadership has been questioned recently, his early work for human rights and democracy remains an example of leadership under challenging contexts.

Elon Musk.

Entrepreneur and CEO of companies such as Tesla and SpaceX, Musk has revolutionized several industries and is known for his vision of a sustainable and interplanetary future. With Tesla, Musk has pioneered the electric automotive industry, promoting the adoption of electric vehicles and renewable energy. Their innovations have had a significant impact on reducing carbon emissions. With SpaceX, Musk has advanced reusable rocket technology, making space exploration more accessible and affordable. His vision of colonizing Mars has captured the imagination and driven new research and development in the space sector.

Angela Merkel.

Chancellor of Germany from 2005 to 2021, she has been an influential leader globally, known for her pragmatic leadership and ability to manage crises. Merkel has demonstrated strong leadership during various crises, including the 2008 financial crisis, the 2015 migrant crisis, and the COVID-19 pandemic. His ability to make difficult decisions and focus on economic and social stability has been widely recognized. Under his leadership, Germany has advanced policies related to renewable energy, social justice, and gender equality. Merkel has promoted European integration and been an essential voice in global politics.

Najib Bukele.

Since 2019, Bukele has been president of El Salvador. He has implemented various reforms and used innovative digital strategies to govern, earning both support and criticism at the national and international levels. Bukele has promoted using digital technologies to improve government transparency and efficiency. His administration has used social media and digital platforms to communicate directly with citizens, which has increased his popularity and perceived accessibility.

It has implemented aggressive security policies to reduce crime rates in El Salvador, including deploying security forces and constructing new prisons. These measures have been effective in reducing homicides, although they have also been criticized for alleged human rights violations. Bukele has pushed for adopting Bitcoin as a legal tender in El Salvador, making the country the first in the world to do so. This move has generated excitement and controversy, with the potential to position El Salvador as an innovative fintech hub with significant economic risks.

Leadership significantly impacts society, shaping the course of communities, nations, and the world at large.

Leaders can transform the reality of the people they serve through inspiration, innovation, promoting justice, stability, and sustainable development. Wangari's examples Maathai, Aung San Suu Kyi, Elon Musk, Angela Merkel, and Nayib Bukele demonstrate how positive leadership can generate lasting and profound changes, inspiring future generations to follow in his footsteps and continue working for a better world.

Chapter 12: Impact of Influencers on Society

The Role of Influencers in Modern Culture.

In the digital age, influencers have significantly shaped modern culture. Influencers can reach global audiences through social media platforms, impact purchasing decisions, and create cultural trends. Their ability to connect directly with followers gives them considerable power to influence opinions, behaviors, and social norms.

Influencers are often pioneers in creating and spreading trends in fashion, beauty, technology, lifestyle, and other fields. Their ability to quickly reach a large audience allows them to introduce and popularize new products, styles, and behaviors.

Brands have recognized the value of influencers as effective marketing and advertising channels. Influencers can personalize and humanize product promotion, making recommendations seem more authentic and trustworthy to their followers.

Many influencers use their platforms to promote social, political, and environmental causes. By doing so, they can raise public awareness and funds and mobilize their supporters to act on various vital issues.

Influencers can empower their followers with knowledge and skills in specific areas through tutorials, tips, and educational content. From cooking and fitness to technology and personal development, influencers provide valuable and accessible resources.

Influencers often create communities around their shared interests and values. These communities provide a sense of belonging and connection between people worldwide, encouraging interaction and mutual support. Below are examples of influencers who have made significant contributions in their respective areas to illustrate the impact of influencers on society.

Huda Kattan.

Founder of Huda Beauty, she is a beauty influencer who has revolutionized the makeup industry.

Kattan used her blog and social media accounts to share makeup tutorials and tips. His authenticity and technical knowledge allowed him to build a loyal fan base. Through her content, Kattan has empowered many people to explore and celebrate their beauty. Additionally, her business success has inspired other women to pursue careers in business and entrepreneurship. The Huda Beauty brand has become one of the most successful makeup brands, known for its innovative and high-quality products.

Nas Daily (Nuseir Yassin).

Nas Daily is a content creator with global recognition for his one-minute videos. Through his videos, Yassin tells stories of people and places worldwide, highlighting diversity and shared humanity. Her videos encourage cultural understanding and empathy. Yassin uses his platform to educate his followers on social, political, and environmental issues. He has created content on climate change, poverty, and human rights, among other topics. The Nas Community Daily has become a space where people can share their stories and connect with others from different cultures and backgrounds.

Liza Koshy.

She is a comedian and influencer who has used her humor and charisma to build a career in entertainment. Koshy has created comedic content that entertains millions on platforms like YouTube and Instagram. His humor and positive energy have provided an escape and joy to his followers. As a woman of Indian and African descent, Koshy has advocated diversity and representation in the media. She has used her platform to promote inclusion and equality. Koshy has also been involved in several philanthropic initiatives, using his influence to support charitable causes and encourage volunteerism.

Lilly Singh (Superwoman).

Also known as Superwoman, she is a comedian, actress, and author who has significantly impacted social media and beyond. Singh has been a trailblazer as one of the first women of South Asian descent to succeed on YouTube and American television. Its success has opened doors for other diverse content creators. Through her content, Singh addresses issues of female empowerment, gender equality, and mental health. His honesty and openness have inspired many of his followers. Singh has used her platform to support various charitable causes, including education for girls and helping disadvantaged communities.

Elise Strachan (My Cupcake Addiction).

She is a cooking influencer known for her YouTube channel, " My Cupcake Addiction," where she shares recipes and baking tutorials. Strachan has taught millions through her detailed and accessible tutorials, making baking fun and achievable for everyone. Her hands-on, educational approach has empowered her followers to develop new culinary skills, encouraging creativity and confidence in the kitchen. Their global community of followers connects through their shared love of baking, creating a positive and supportive space on social media.

Influencers play a crucial role in modern culture, impacting various areas, from fashion and beauty to education and social justice. Through their platforms, they can create trends, promote essential causes, and connect people worldwide. The examples of Huda Kattan, Nas Daily, Liza Koshy, Lilly Singh, and Elise Strachan demonstrate how influencers can use their reach and influence to make meaningful contributions to society, inspiring and empowering their followers and creating positive change.

Chapter 13: Transformational Leadership

Concept and Characteristics of Transformational Leadership.

Transformational leadership is an approach in which leaders inspire and motivate their followers to transcend their interests to achieve a greater good and transform their capabilities and values. This leadership style focuses on creating positive and meaningful change in organizations and followers' lives, guiding them to higher performance and morality.

Transformational leaders have a clear and compelling vision of the future. This vision inspires followers and motivates them to work enthusiastically and be dedicated to common goals. Communicating this vision effectively is crucial to aligning all organization members toward a shared goal.

These leaders motivate their followers to strive beyond their normal expectations. They use inspiration, enthusiasm, and charisma to encourage followers to commit to the organization's mission and values fully. This type of motivation goes beyond extrinsic rewards and focuses on personal and professional growth.

Transformational leadership involves paying attention to followers' individual needs and aspirations. Transformational leaders act as mentors or coaches, providing support, advice, and personal development opportunities. They recognize and value everyone's unique contribution, fostering an environment of respect and empowerment.

Transformational leaders foster an environment where followers feel challenged to think critically and creatively. They promote innovation and question the status quo, encouraging followers to seek new solutions to problems. This approach enables continuous learning and adaptability within the organization.

Ethics and values are fundamental in transformational leadership. These leaders operate with integrity and adhere to high moral and ethical standards. They set an example for their followers to follow, demonstrating behaviors that reflect the organization's values and promoting a culture of transparency and fairness.

In today's context, where uncertainty and rapid change are constant and where perceptions of what is good or bad can vary widely, transformational leaders are more important than ever. There are many reasons why this leadership style is crucial in a turbulent and changing world:

Adaptability and Resilience. Transformational leadership fosters adaptability and resilience in times of change. Leaders who practice this style are equipped to guide their followers through difficult and complex situations, keeping them focused on the long-term vision and helping them adapt to new realities.

Moral and Ethical Clarity. Transformational leaders provide moral and ethical clarity in a world where definitions of right and wrong can be confusing or shifting. By adhering to strong principles and consistent values, these leaders establish a clear framework for decision-making and organizational behavior, protecting the integrity and reputation of the organization.

Inspiration in Times of Disillusionment. Transformational leaders can inspire and revitalize their followers in times of disappointment or demoralization. Her focus on higher purpose and personal growth helps people find meaning and motivation even in adverse situations.

Promotion of Innovation and Positive Change. In an environment where change is constant, the ability to innovate is essential. Transformational leaders foster a culture of innovation by encouraging followers to explore new ideas and challenge the status quo. This approach drives progress within the organization and allows the organization to remain competitive and relevant.

Creation of Cohesive Communities. Transformational leaders can unite people around a shared vision and values. In a fragmented world, this ability to build cohesive communities is invaluable. By fostering inclusion, respect, and collaboration, these leaders create environments where all members feel valued and committed to collective success.

Development of Future Leaders. A distinctive characteristic of transformational leaders is their focus on developing future leaders. By acting as mentors and role models, these leaders ensure the continuity of organizational culture and values, preparing the next generation to take on leadership roles and meet future challenges.

Transformational leadership is a powerful and necessary approach in the modern world. Transformational leaders create positive, lasting change by inspiring, motivating, and guiding their followers toward personal and professional growth. In a turbulent and changing world, where perceptions of right and wrong can be ambiguous, these leaders provide moral clarity, foster innovation, and help people and organizations adapt and thrive. Their ability to build cohesive communities and develop future leaders ensures that organizations survive and thrive well into the future.

Chapter 14: Influencers as Agents of Change

Influencers have emerged as potent social and cultural change agents in the digital age. With the ability to reach global audiences and mobilize thousands or even millions of people, influencers can play a crucial role in promoting ideas, values, and social movements. There are many ways that influencers can promote significant change:

Influencers can amplify causes and issues that may need more attention in traditional media. By using their platforms to highlight important topics such as climate change, social justice, human rights, and mental health, influencers can raise awareness and educate their followers about these issues. This visibility can generate greater public interest and foster crucial discussions.

Through fundraising campaigns, charity events, and calls to action, influencers can mobilize resources and actions supporting various causes. Influencers can make a tangible impact in their communities and beyond by using their platforms to organize donation drives or encourage their followers to participate in events or protests.

Influencers can promote positive and sustainable behaviors among their followers. Whether promoting healthy living practices, environmental sustainability, or inclusion and diversity, influencers can serve as role models, demonstrating how small actions can contribute to positive change. Their ability to influence people's behavior allows them to promote habits and attitudes that benefit individuals and society.

Many influencers use their platform to challenge social norms and stereotypes perpetuating discrimination and inequality. By sharing their experiences and perspectives, influencers can challenge dominant narratives and promote a more inclusive and diverse view of society. This may include fighting to promote racial equality or the defense of human rights, to name a few.

Influencers often create online communities that provide support and a sense of belonging to their followers. These communities can be safe spaces where people feel understood and validated and can find emotional support and resources. By building these communities, influencers can help their followers navigate personal and social challenges, promoting resilience and empowerment.

Influencers use various strategies to maximize their influence and generate a significant impact. They often create educational and informative content to raise awareness and educate their followers on essential topics. This can include social media posts, videos, blogs, and podcasts that explain key concepts, provide data and statistics, and offer practical advice. By providing accessible and reliable information, influencers can empower their followers to make informed decisions.

Collaborations with other public figures, charities, NGOs, and companies can amplify an influencer's impact. By working together, influencers and their partners can reach new audiences, combine resources and expertise, and organize more effective campaigns. These alliances can also increase the influencer's credibility and strengthen their message.

Sharing personal stories and testimonials can be a powerful way to connect with followers and build empathy. Influencers often share their experiences to illustrate how a specific topic has affected them and why it is essential. These stories can make complex issues more understandable and emotional, mobilizing followers to act.

Hashtags and viral movements effectively unite people around a common cause. By creating or promoting specific hashtags, influencers can make engaging and amplifying a campaign's reach easier for their followers. These moves can attract media attention and generate additional momentum for the cause.

Transparency and authenticity are crucial to building and maintaining follower trust. Influencers who are open and honest about their motivations and experiences often have a more profound and lasting impact. By demonstrating a genuine commitment to a cause and being transparent about their relationships with brands and organizations, influencers can strengthen their credibility and foster a relationship of trust with their audience.

Influencers use multiple social media platforms and communication channels to maximize their reach. These include Instagram, YouTube, Twitter, TikTok, blogs, and podcasts. By adapting their message to different formats and audiences, influencers can reach a broader and more diverse follower base, ensuring their message has the most significant impact.

Influencers are crucial as social and cultural change agents in the modern world. Through their ability to raise awareness, mobilize resources, promote positive behaviors, challenge social norms, and create supportive communities, influencers can make a significant and lasting impact. Influencers can amplify their influence and encourage positive societal changes by employing educational content creation, collaborations, personal stories, hashtag campaigns, transparency, and multiple platforms. Their ability to connect with people on an emotional and personal level makes them a powerful force for social and cultural good.

Chapter 15: Leadership in Times of Crisis

Leadership in crisis is a crucial skill that can determine the success or failure of an organization, community, or nation. During emergencies, leaders face exceptional challenges that require quick decisions, clear communication, and excellent adaptability. Below are some of the key strategies and approaches that leaders use to manage and overcome crises:

Clear and transparent communication is essential in a crisis. Leaders must provide accurate and timely information to all stakeholders, including employees, customers, citizens, and the media. Communication should be consistent and truthful, helping to prevent the spread of rumors and misunderstandings. Furthermore, transparency in decision-making generates trust and peace of mind in times of uncertainty.

During a crisis, time is of the essence. Influential leaders must make quick, decisive decisions based on the best information available. Although it is crucial to act quickly, it is also essential to carefully evaluate the options and consider the possible consequences of each decision. The ability to remain calm under pressure and act with determination is vital.

Crises often involve changing conditions and unforeseen scenarios. Leaders must be flexible and adaptable, willing to adjust their strategies and plans in response to new information or circumstances. This adaptability allows you to respond effectively to emerging challenges and prepares the organization to navigate an uncertain and volatile environment.

Empathy is a crucial quality for leaders in times of crisis. Leaders must know their followers' emotions and needs and be willing to provide support and understanding. This includes recognizing and validating feelings of anxiety, fear, or frustration and offering resources and assistance to help people cope. Empathy helps strengthen morale and team spirit.

A crisis often requires a coordinated and collaborative response. Leaders must work effectively with different groups and organizations, including government agencies, NGOs, businesses, and the wider community. This collaboration is crucial for sharing resources, information, and experiences and ensuring a unified and coherent response.

Leaders in crisis must focus on finding practical and feasible solutions to their problems. This involves an action-oriented mindset, seeking opportunities to solve problems innovatively and efficiently. Additionally, leaders must foster resilience at the individual and organizational levels, helping people recover from adversity and prepare for future challenges.

Examples of Effective Leadership During Emergency Situations.

Winston Churchill, Prime Minister of the United Kingdom during World War II, is widely recognized for his effective leadership during one of the greatest crises in modern history. Churchill was a master orator and used his speeches to inspire and motivate the British people in the darkest moments of the war. His famous speech, " We shall fight on the beaches," exemplifies how he used language to unify and strengthen national morale. He made critical strategic decisions, such as the defense of Britain against the Nazi invasion and the alliance with the United States and the Soviet Union. His decisive leadership was crucial to the eventual victory of the Allies.

Jacinda Ardern, Prime Minister of New Zealand, has been praised internationally for handling the COVID-19 pandemic. Ardern has been transparent and communicative with the public, providing regular and clear updates on the situation and necessary measures. His empathetic approach and calming tone have effectively built trust and maintained public calm. New Zealand implemented strict lockdown and border control measures quickly, effectively controlling the virus's spread. These quick, science-based decisions helped minimize the impact of the virus on public health and the economy.

Rudy Giuliani, then mayor of New York, played a crucial role during the terrorist attacks of September 11, 2001. Giuliani was present at the scene, providing visible and reassuring leadership. His ability to communicate clearly and calmly helped coordinate the emergency response and maintain order. Coordination and Collaboration: Giuliani worked closely with emergency agencies, police, and firefighters to organize an adequate response. He also facilitated collaboration with federal and state agencies, ensuring a coordinated response to the crisis.

Angela Merkel, Chancellor of Germany, showed decisive leadership during the European migration crisis in 2015. Merkel decided to open Germany's borders to refugees fleeing war and persecution, which was a controversial but humanitarian measure. His decision was based on principles of human rights and solidarity. Communication and Public Opinion Management: Although she faced criticism and political challenges, Merkel handled the situation with clear communication and a strong defense of her policies. His pragmatic approach helped stabilize the situation and integrate the refugees into German society.

Leadership in times of crisis requires a combination of skills and qualities that enable leaders to guide their organizations and communities through exceptional challenges. Clear communication, quick decision-making, flexibility, empathy, and collaboration are critical to managing crises effectively. The examples of Winston Churchill, Jacinda Ardern, Rudy Giuliani, and Angela Merkel highlight how effective leadership can make a crucial difference in managing emergencies, providing solutions to immediate problems, and inspiring hope in difficult times.

Chapter 16: Personal Growth Strategies for Leaders

Personal growth is essential for leaders who want to improve their skills and effectiveness. Specific techniques and practices can help leaders develop their capabilities, increase self-confidence, and better guide their teams and organizations.

Self-assessment and regular reflection are essential for personal growth. Leaders should take the time to evaluate their strengths, weaknesses, and areas for improvement. This may include using assessment tools such as 360-degree feedback, self-assessment surveys, or personal reflection on past experiences and challenges. Reflection helps leaders understand their patterns of behavior and identify development opportunities.

Setting clear and achievable goals is a crucial practice for personal growth. Leaders must define specific, measurable, attainable, relevant, and time-bound (SMART) objectives. These goals may encompass communication skills, time management, conflict resolution, or technical skill development. Setting goals helps maintain focus and motivation and provides a framework for measuring progress.

Education and continuing training are essential for leadership development. Leaders must be committed to constant learning and participate in courses, workshops, seminars, and leadership development programs. This enhances knowledge and skills and provides new perspectives and problem-solving approaches.

Seeking guidance from mentors and coaches is an effective strategy for personal growth. Mentors can offer advice based on their experience and provide support and guidance in decision-making. Coaches, on the other hand, can help leaders develop specific skills and work on areas of improvement through structured, personalized sessions.

Effective communication is a critical skill for any leader. Improving communication skills, such as active listening, public speaking, and writing, is essential for personal leadership. Leaders must learn to express their ideas clearly and persuasively and to listen and respond to the concerns of others constructively.

Effective time management and productivity are critical skills for leadership success. Leaders must learn to prioritize tasks, delegate responsibilities, and use time management tools to optimize efficiency. Healthy routines and habits, such as daily planning and eliminating distractions, can also improve productivity.

Emotional intelligence is the ability to recognize and manage one's own emotions and those of others. It is a vital leadership skill that allows leaders to manage stress, decision-making, and interpersonal relationships more effectively. Developing emotional intelligence involves improving self-awareness, self-regulation, empathy, and relationship management skills.

Personal well-being and work-life balance are critical to sustainable leadership. Leaders should care for their physical and mental health, incorporating regular exercise, meditation, proper nutrition, and sufficient rest. Maintaining a healthy work-life balance helps prevent burnout and maintain energy and focus.

Self-awareness and continuous development are essential components of personal growth and effective leadership.

Self-knowledge is the basis of personal growth. Leaders who understand their values, beliefs, strengths, and weaknesses are better equipped to make decisions aligned with their principles and goals. Self-awareness also allows leaders to recognize how their emotions and behaviors affect others, which is crucial for empathy and relationship management.

Continuous development allows leaders to remain adaptable and flexible in a changing environment. Learning and adapting is critical in a rapidly evolving world of technologies, business practices, and social expectations. Leaders who commit to continuous learning can respond more effectively to new challenges and opportunities.

Self-knowledge and continuous development improve decision-making. By understanding their biases, limitations, and areas for improvement, leaders can make more informed and balanced decisions. Additionally, by staying abreast of the latest trends and insights in their field, they can make strategic decisions that benefit their organizations.

Emotional intelligence and empathy, developed through self-knowledge, are vital to building and maintaining healthy interpersonal relationships. Leaders who understand their own emotions and those of others can communicate more effectively, resolve conflicts, and create a positive, collaborative work environment.

Commitment to personal development not only benefits the leader but also his followers. Leaders who demonstrate a commitment to growth and continuous improvement are role models, inspiring and motivating others to do the same. This can create an organizational culture of learning and development where all members feel empowered to reach their full potential.

Continuous development and self-awareness help leaders build resilience. When faced with challenges and failures, resilient leaders can learn from their experiences and bounce back stronger. This resilience is crucial to maintaining motivation and focus during times of uncertainty or difficulty.

Personal growth is a continuous process and essential for effective leadership. Leaders can improve their effectiveness and well-being through techniques and practices such as self-assessment, goal setting, continuing education, mentoring, and developing communication and time management skills. Self-awareness and a commitment to continuous development enable leaders to adapt to change, make informed decisions, and build healthy relationships, all critical to inspiring and guiding others. By investing in personal growth, leaders improve their leadership capacity and contribute to their organizations' and communities' success and sustainability

Chapter 17: Personal Growth Strategies for Influencers

In the dynamic and competitive world of social media, influencers face the constant challenge of maintaining their relevance and authenticity. As trends and audience expectations change, influencers must find ways to connect with their followers and adapt to new demands genuinely. Below are key strategies to help influencers stay relevant and authentic:

To stay relevant, influencers must understand their audience and be in tune with their interests, needs, and preferences. This involves conducting regular research, engaging with followers through comments and surveys, and analyzing performance data to identify what content resonates best. By tailoring content to audience interests, influencers can stay relevant and engaging.

Creativity is essential to stand out in an environment saturated with content. Influencers must constantly look for new ideas and formats to present their content freshly and attractively. This may include using new platforms, innovative video formats, collaborations with other influencers or experts, and experimenting with different visual and narrative styles. Innovation helps capture the attention and maintain the interest of the audience.

Authenticity is a crucial value in influencer marketing. Followers value honesty and transparency and are more likely to trust influencers who come across as genuine. This means being honest about paid collaborations, sharing personal experiences, and communicating authentically. Influencers must be true to their values and avoid compromising their authenticity for popularity or financial benefits.

Continued personal and professional growth is not just a necessity but a source of inspiration for influencers. It's essential to staying relevant in the ever-evolving landscape of influencer marketing. By investing in their education and development and attending workshops, courses, and conferences, influencers can learn about new trends, technologies, and best practices. This continuous learning journey not only keeps them informed and up to date but also inspires them to offer valuable and relevant content to their audience.

Social media platforms and digital technologies are constantly evolving. Influencers must be willing to explore and adopt new platforms and tools to reach new audiences and stay competitive. This includes being aware of new platform features and being open to experimenting with emerging platforms.

Authenticity is also crucial in relationships with brands. Influencers should collaborate with brands that align with their values and are relevant to their audience. To maintain followers' trust, it is essential to be selective and not accept all collaboration offers—genuine partnerships with brands the influencer supports are perceived as more authentic and credible.

Techniques to Manage Mental Health and Wellbeing.

Being an influencer can be a rewarding career, but it also presents significant challenges to mental health and wellbeing. The pressure to maintain a public image, constant exposure to criticism, and the need to always be "on" can negatively impact emotional and psychological well-being. Below are techniques and strategies to help influencers manage their mental health and well-being:

Establishing clear boundaries between professional and personal life is crucial and a form of self-care for influencers. This includes setting work and rest schedules and limiting screen time to avoid burnout. Influencers need to know when to disconnect and take time for themselves without constantly feeling obligated to be available online. This balance and self-care are essential for maintaining mental health and well-being in the demanding world of influencer marketing.

Self-care is essential to maintaining mental health and well-being. This may include regular exercise, meditation, healthy eating, and adequate sleep. Influencers should spend time doing activities that help them relax and recharge.

Managing stress and anxiety is essential in a career that can be very demanding. Influencers can benefit from deep breathing, mindfulness meditation, and yoga. Learning time management and task delegation techniques to reduce workload and stress is also helpful. Influencers mustn't feel alone in their challenges. Seeking support from friends, family, or mental health professionals can be very beneficial. Therapy or coaching can offer tools and strategies to manage stress and emotional difficulties. Additionally, belonging to a supportive community, whether online or in person, can provide a safe space to share experiences and receive support.

Social media can be a source of comparison and stress. Influencers should develop a healthy relationship with these platforms, avoid constantly comparing themselves to others, and recognize that social media does not always represent the whole reality. Taking regular breaks from social media and limiting content consumption can help maintain a balanced perspective.

Influencers must recognize and accept that they cannot always be perfect or please everyone. Accepting imperfection and failure as part of growth is critical to maintaining healthy self-esteem. Learning from mistakes and being kind to yourself in difficult times is essential for mental well-being.

Personal growth is essential for influencers to maintain relevance and authenticity in an ever-changing environment. Influencers can remain influential and trusted by knowing their audience, being innovative, transparent, and authentic, and committing to continuous learning. At the same time, influencers must manage their mental health and well-being by setting boundaries, practicing self-care, managing stress, and seeking emotional support. Influencers can enjoy a rewarding and sustainable career by balancing professional success with personal well-being.

Chapter 18: Leadership in the Digital Age

How Technology Has Transformed Leadership.

Digital technology has revolutionized virtually every aspect of modern life, including leadership. Digitalization has changed how leaders communicate, manage teams, make decisions, and execute strategies. Here are the key ways technology has transformed leadership:

Digital tools have facilitated more efficient and transparent communication between leaders and their teams. Platforms such as emails, instant messaging applications, and video conferencing tools allow for fast and direct communication regardless of geographic location. Collaboration platforms, such as Slack or Microsoft Teams, enable teams to work together in real time, sharing information and documents seamlessly.

The digital age has provided leaders with unprecedented access to data and information. Data analysis, artificial intelligence, and big data tools allow leaders to make more informed and evidence-based decisions. Leaders can analyze market trends, consumer behavior, and performance metrics to adjust strategies and improve operational efficiency.

Technology has made remote work possible, transforming how leaders manage their teams. Project management platforms like Asana or Trello and video conferencing allow leaders to coordinate distributed teams and maintain productivity. This flexibility also allows organizations to attract and retain talent worldwide.

Technology drives innovation and digital transformation within organizations. Leaders must be aware of emerging technologies, such as artificial intelligence, automation, and blockchain, and consider how they can be integrated into their business models. Leading digital transformation is now a critical competency for modern leaders.

Digital platforms have made more inclusive leadership possible. Social media and other communication platforms allow leaders to interact directly with stakeholders, including employees, customers, and communities. This encourages a greater diversity of opinions and perspectives, improving decision-making and innovation.

Challenges and Opportunities of Leadership in the Digital World.

Leadership in the digital age presents both unique challenges and opportunities. One of the most significant challenges of digital leadership is information overload. With the vast amount of data available, it can be difficult for leaders to filter relevant information and make informed decisions. Leaders must develop skills to effectively manage and analyze data and use artificial intelligence tools to process large volumes of information.

Accessing and analyzing data allows leaders to make more accurate, evidence-based decisions. Using predictive analytics and data models, leaders can identify emerging trends, anticipate problems, and confidently make strategic decisions.

Digitalization also presents risks related to data security and privacy. Cyberattacks and data breaches can have severe consequences for organizations. Through robust security measures and cybersecurity practices, leaders must protect their systems and data.

Cybersecurity is an opportunity for innovation. Leaders can invest in advanced security technologies, such as data encryption and multi-factor authentication, and in employee training on security best practices. Protecting the organization's data can become a competitive advantage.

Managing remote and multigenerational teams presents unique challenges. Lack of face-to-face interaction can make building relationships and team cohesion difficult. Additionally, generational differences can lead to different approaches to technology and work.

Remote and diverse teams offer a wealth of perspectives and experiences. Leaders can leverage this diversity to foster innovation and creativity. Additionally, the flexibility of remote work can improve employee satisfaction and retention and allow organizations to access global talent.

Maintaining a consistent organizational culture can be difficult in a digital environment. Lack of physical presence can make employees feel disconnected from the organization's values and goals.

Leaders can use digital tools to reinforce organizational culture, such as internal communication platforms, virtual events, and online recognition programs. Regular communication and celebrating achievements can help maintain a sense of community and shared purpose.

The rapid evolution of technology requires leaders to adapt continually. This can be challenging, as new technologies may require new skills and approaches.

Continuous adaptation is also an opportunity for learning and professional development. Leaders must foster a culture of constant learning within their organizations, encouraging employees to update their skills and knowledge. This improves the organization's ability to adapt to change and motivates and retains employees.

Leadership in the digital age presents a unique set of challenges and opportunities. Technology has transformed how leaders communicate, make decisions, and manage teams. While information overload, data security, and managing remote teams are significant challenges, there are opportunities for data-driven decision-making, cybersecurity innovation, and workplace diversity. Leaders who can adapt to these changes and take advantage of the opportunities of the digital world will be better prepared to lead their organizations to success in the future. By fostering a continuous learning and adaptability culture, leaders can ensure their organizations are resilient and competitive in a constantly evolving environment.

Chapter 19: The Power of Narrative in Leadership

Storytelling is a powerful tool in leadership, used to inspire, motivate, and communicate effectively. Leaders who master the art of storytelling can connect with their followers on an emotional level, convey values and visions, and foster a sense of shared purpose. Explored here are the ways leaders use stories to strengthen their leadership:

Stories are an effective way to communicate an organization's or community's vision and values. Through stories, leaders can illustrate what the organization stands for, what is essential, and where it is going. Stories incorporating the mission and core values help followers understand and align with the organization's broader purpose.

Stories have the power to connect people on an emotional level. Leaders who share personal or moving stories can generate empathy and understanding among their followers. This emotional connection is vital to building relationships of trust and loyalty, motivating people to commit and collaborate.

Stories of overcoming, success, and resilience can be powerful sources of inspiration and motivation. Leaders can motivate their followers to persevere and aspire for greatness by sharing examples of challenges overcome or goals achieved. These stories serve as role models and show that overcoming obstacles and achieving success is possible.

Stories can simplify complex concepts and make them more accessible. Leaders can use metaphors, analogies, and narratives to explain complicated ideas in a way that is easy to understand and remember. This is especially useful when communicating strategies, organizational changes, or new projects.

Stories can also be a tool for changing mindsets and behaviors. By presenting examples of people or groups that have adopted new ways of thinking or acting, leaders can influence their followers to do the same. Stories highlighting the benefits of change or the risks of not changing can be incredibly persuasive.

Stories that reflect the organization's successes and challenges can reinforce organizational culture. Celebrating collective achievement, innovation, or customer service stories can strengthen team identity and spirit. At the same time, sharing stories of mistakes and lessons learned can foster a culture of continuous learning and improvement.

Nelson Mandela, leader of the anti-apartheid movement in South Africa, used the narrative of the fight for freedom and justice to unite his nation. His autobiography, "Long Walk to Freedom," and his speeches were powerful tools for the story of resistance against oppression and the fight for equality. Mandela used his own experience of imprisonment as a symbol of sacrifice and resistance, inspiring millions to join the cause for freedom and justice.

Steve Jobs, co-founder of Apple, mastered using narrative to inspire and motivate. In his product launch speeches, such as the famous iPhone launch in 2007, Jobs introduced new technologies and told a story about how these products would transform people's lives. He used stories of innovation and creativity to position Apple as a company that challenges the status quo and leads the future of technology.

Have a Dream " speech is one of the most iconic examples of storytelling in leadership. King used a powerful story of a future where people would be judged by their character and not the color of their skin. This speech inspired civil rights activists in the United States and mobilized people worldwide to fight for equality and justice.

Sheryl Sandberg, Facebook's COO and author of Lean In, has used her narrative to address issues of gender and leadership in the workplace. By sharing her experience of facing barriers as a woman in leadership positions, Sandberg has motivated women worldwide to "come to the table" and seek leadership opportunities. Her story of overcoming personal and professional challenges has resonated with many people, fostering a global movement for gender equality.

Malala Yousafzai, a young Pakistani activist, has used her experience to advocate for girls' education rights. She survived a Taliban attack for advocating for girls' education and later co-wrote the book "I Am Malala." His story has raised awareness in the international community about the importance of education and inspired many to support his cause. Her narrative of courage and resilience is a powerful example of how one voice can create global change.

The power of narrative in leadership cannot be underestimated. Through stories, leaders can communicate visions and values, inspire and motivate, and connect emotionally with their followers. Stories can simplify complex concepts, change mindsets, and reinforce organizational culture. The examples of Nelson Mandela, Steve Jobs, Martin Luther King Jr., Sheryl Sandberg, and Malala Yousafzai demonstrate how powerful narratives can mobilize people, create movements, and create meaningful change. For leaders, mastering the art of storytelling is an invaluable skill that can help guide their followers toward a better future.

Chapter 20: The Power of Narrative in Influencers

In the digital sphere, influencers have found storytelling a powerful tool to connect with followers, build brands, and promote products or causes. The ability to tell stories effectively allows influencers to stand out in a saturated space and maintain their audience's interest. Below explores how influencers create and share compelling stories:

Influencers often create authentic and personal stories, allowing them to connect emotionally with their audience. Sharing personal experiences, both positive and negative, helps followers see the influencer as a natural, relatable person. Vulnerability in stories, such as about personal struggles or challenges overcome, can strengthen the relationship between the influencer and their audience, fostering empathy and loyalty.

Influencers often base their stories on everyday situations and shared experiences that their followers can easily understand. By sharing stories from their daily lives, whether it's fashion, beauty, fitness, cooking, or travel, influencers make their content relevant and accessible. These narratives can inspire followers to try new things or adopt certain habits or products.

Influencers use narrative to build a coherent, consistent identity that reflects their values, interests, and lifestyle. This identity is communicated through all the platforms and content they share. A consistent narrative helps establish a solid and differentiated personal brand, making it easier for followers to understand what the influencer stands for and what they can expect from their content.

Influencer stories are often presented in visual and multimedia formats, harnessing the power of images, videos, and graphics. Platforms like Instagram, YouTube, and TikTok allow influencers to combine text, photos, and music to create engaging and dynamic narratives. This creative use of multimedia not only captures attention but also enriches the narrative experience for the audience.

To maintain audience interest and engagement, influencers often incorporate elements of suspense and surprise into their stories. This may include unexpected revelations, plot twists, or the promise of exclusive content in the future. These elements keep the audience interested and eager for more, increasing engagement and follower retention.

Influencers engage their audience in their stories, encouraging interaction and participation. This may include direct questions, surveys, contests, or requests for comments and opinions. By making the audience feel part of the narrative, influencers strengthen the connection and loyalty of their followers.

Storytelling Techniques Used by Successful Influencers.

Influencers use narrative arcs to structure their stories, giving them a beginning, a middle, and an end. This may include presenting a problem or challenge, describing the overcoming or resolution process, and describing the result or lesson learned. Narrative arcs help give coherence and direction to stories, keeping the audience engaged over time.

Influencers often position themselves as protagonists of their stories but can also include other characters, such as friends, family, or pets. These characters add depth and context to stories and can help convey messages or values more effectively. The presence of identifiable characters allows followers to see themselves reflected in the stories.

Stories that evoke emotions, such as joy, sadness, hope, or empathy, are compelling. Influencers use emotional messages to connect with their audience on a deeper level. This may include sharing emotional moments or talking about important causes. Emotional stories are memorable and can have a lasting impact on the audience.

Maintaining thematic consistency is crucial for influencer storytelling. This means the shared stories must align with the influencer's core themes and values, such as wellness, sustainable fashion, social activism, or adventure. Thematic consistency helps reinforce the influencer's brand and attract an audience with those interests.

Interactive storytelling involves using tools and platforms that allow the audience to participate actively in the story. This can include polls on Instagram Stories, live Q&As, or the creation of user-generated content. Interactive storytelling increases engagement and provides valuable feedback and a connection with the audience.

Transformation narratives show a significant change in the influencer or someone they relate to. This could be a personal transformation, such as a weight loss journey, a career change, or achieving a goal. These stories inspire audiences by demonstrating that change is possible and showing the path to attain similar goals.

The power of storytelling is an invaluable tool for influencers in the digital age. Influencers can build a deep connection with their audience, communicate their values, and promote products or causes through authentic, personal, and emotionally resonant stories. Storytelling techniques, such as creating narrative arcs, using characters, and integrating emotional messages, allow influencers to capture and maintain the attention of their followers. Additionally, interactive storytelling and thematic consistency strengthen the relationship with the audience and reinforce personal brand identity. In a saturated digital environment, mastering storytelling is essential to stand out and have a lasting impact as an influencer.

Chapter 21: Leadership and Social Responsibility

Leadership and social responsibility are intrinsically linked, as leaders are crucial in promoting ethical and sustainable practices within their organizations and society. Social responsibility refers to the obligation of companies and organizations to act for the benefit of humanity and the environment beyond their economic interests. Below, explore ways leaders can promote social responsibility:

Leaders must define a clear vision of social responsibility that reflects the organization's values and principles. This vision must communicate the company's commitment to ethics, sustainability, and social well-being. Leaders must ensure this vision is integrated into the organization's mission and strategy and communicated effectively at all levels.

Leaders are responsible for implementing sustainable practices throughout the company's operations. This includes adopting policies and procedures that minimize environmental impact, such as waste reduction, efficient resource use, and renewable energy promotion. Leaders must foster a culture of sustainability, encouraging employees to participate in green initiatives and be aware of the impact of their actions.

Ethics and transparency are fundamental pillars of social responsibility. Leaders must establish and maintain high ethical standards, ensuring that all business practices are fair and legal. This includes transparency in communication with employees, customers, investors, and the community. Leaders must also be open and honest about company practices, including resource management, decision-making, and social and environmental impact.

Leaders can promote social responsibility by investing in community and social welfare initiatives. These can include volunteer programs, donations to charitable causes, and support for education and skills development. By contributing to the community's well-being, leaders help improve people's quality of life and strengthen the company's reputation and relationship with the community.

Diversity and inclusion are critical components of social responsibility. Leaders must promote an organizational culture that values and respects diversity in all its forms, including gender, race, sexual orientation, disability, and more. This involves implementing policies and practices that ensure equal opportunity and fair treatment for all employees. Diversity and inclusion enhance innovation and creativity and reflect a commitment to social justice.

Leaders must establish metrics to evaluate and measure the social impact of their social responsibility initiatives. This involves tracking key performance indicators (KPIs) related to sustainability, employee well-being, diversity, and other social aspects. By measuring impact, leaders can identify areas for improvement and adjust their strategies to maximize social and environmental benefits.

Examples of Social Responsibility Initiatives Led by Companies and Organizations.

Patagonia and Environmental Sustainability.

Patagonia, an outdoor clothing and equipment company, is known for its strong commitment to environmental sustainability. The company has implemented several initiatives, including using recycled materials, reducing the use of water and chemicals in production, and promoting the repair and reuse of products. Patagonia also donates 1% of its sales to environmental causes through its "1% for the Planet." These actions have reduced the company's environmental impact and inspired others in the industry to adopt more sustainable practices.

Ben & Jerry's and Social Justice.

Ben & Jerry's, an ice cream brand, has actively advocated social justice and human rights. The company has used its platform to advocate for marriage equality, racial justice, and reform of the criminal justice system. Additionally, Ben & Jerry's partners with suppliers who meet high ethical and fair trade standards. These initiatives have helped raise awareness of critical social issues and demonstrated the company's commitment to equality and justice. Ben & Jerry's has used its brand voice to influence social change and promote action among its customers and the community.

One " Business Model for One ."

One Business Model." for One, "where the company donates a pair to a person in need for every pair of shoes sold. This initiative has expanded to include other areas, such as providing clean water, healthcare, and vision aid for disadvantaged communities. The " One " model for One " has significantly impacted millions of pairs of shoes and other essential resources for people in more than 70 countries. TOMS has demonstrated how a socially responsible business model can generate a positive impact while being profitable.

Starbucks and Workplace Inclusion.

Starbucks has implemented several initiatives to promote workplace inclusion and diversity. The company is committed to hiring military veterans, refugees, and youth without access to job opportunities. Additionally, Starbucks offers its employees mental health, education, and wellness benefits. These initiatives have improved inclusion and access to opportunities for diverse groups of people. Additionally, by investing in the well-being of its employees, Starbucks has improved morale and job satisfaction, contributing to a more positive and productive work environment.

Microsoft and Sustainability and Accessibility.

Microsoft has committed to being carbon-negative by 2030, meaning it will remove more carbon than it emits. The company also works on accessibility initiatives, developing technologies that allow people with disabilities to access its products and services. Microsoft's sustainability initiatives are helping to reduce the company's environmental impact and lead the technology industry toward greener practices. At the same time, its accessibility efforts are improving inclusion and enabling more people to participate fully in the digital economy.

Leadership in promoting social responsibility is essential for sustainable development and the well-being of society. Leaders are responsible for integrating ethical and sustainable practices into their organizations, fostering a culture of transparency, diversity, and inclusion. Initiatives such as Patagonia, Ben & Jerry's, TOMS, Starbucks, and Microsoft demonstrate how companies can use their influence to generate a positive and lasting impact. By taking an active role in social responsibility, leaders contribute to a better world and strengthen their organization's reputation and long-term success.

Chapter 22: Influencers and Social Responsibility

Influencers have significant power to promote social causes because they can reach large audiences and connect emotionally with their followers. Using their platforms, they can raise awareness of social issues, mobilize resources and actions, and encourage behavioral and attitudinal changes. Below are ways influencers can promote social causes:

Influencers can use their platforms to raise awareness about social issues and educate their followers about essential topics such as gender equality, climate change, mental health, and social justice. Influencers can inform their audience and foster a greater understanding of these issues by sharing information, data, and resources. This is particularly effective when influencers use their voices and experiences to connect emotionally with their followers.

Influencers can advocate for human and social rights, using their platform to support policies and practices that promote justice and equality. This may include participating in activism campaigns, signing petitions, attending protests, and collaborating with nonprofit organizations. Influencers can help generate social and political pressure to address systemic issues by using their influence to advocate for change.

Influencers can be instrumental in raising funds for social causes. They can organize fundraising campaigns on social media platforms, promote charities, and motivate their followers to donate. Additionally, they can mobilize non-monetary resources, such as food, clothing, or volunteerism, to support needy communities.

Influencers can influence their followers' behavior and lifestyle by promoting sustainable and responsible practices. This may include encouraging recycling, responsible consumption, adopting more sustainable diets, or promoting ethical brands. By modeling these behaviors, influencers can inspire followers to make more conscious and moral decisions daily.

Influencers can create a sense of community and solidarity around social causes. By sharing stories of individuals affected by specific issues and highlighting collective efforts to address these issues, influencers can build a community of followers committed to positive change. This strengthens the cause and provides the participants with emotional support and a sense of belonging.

Examples of Successful Social Responsibility Campaigns Led by Influencers.

Leonardo DiCaprio and Environmental Conservation.

Leonardo DiCaprio, actor and environmental activist, has used his platform to raise awareness about environmental conservation and climate change. He has supported projects and organizations that protect biodiversity, oceans, and indigenous rights through the Leonardo DiCaprio Foundation. DiCaprio has raised millions of dollars for environmental causes and produced documentaries such as " Before the Flood," which explore the impacts of climate change. Their activism has helped educate the public about the importance of conservation and mobilized support for global environmental initiatives.

Lizzo and Body Inclusivity.

Lizzo, a singer and activist, has been a vocal advocate for body inclusivity and acceptance of all body types. She uses her social media and performances to promote messages of self-love and acceptance, challenging traditional beauty standards. Lizzo has inspired many people to feel comfortable and confident in their bodies, regardless of conventional beauty standards. Her influence has helped change the conversation about body image and self-esteem, promoting a more inclusive and optimistic view of the body.

Alexander Otaola and the Fight for Democracy in Cuba.

Alexander Otaola, a Cuban presenter and activist, has used his social media platforms and his "Hola! Ota - Ola" program to advocate for democracy and human rights in Cuba. She has been a strong voice against the Cuban regime and has promoted freedom of expression and denunciation of political repression. Otaola has mobilized the Cuban diaspora and other international supporters to support the fight for democracy in Cuba. His activism has helped raise public awareness of the situation in Cuba and has pressured political leaders to act in favor of democracy and human rights.

Rosa María Payá and the Fight for Democracy in Cuba.

Rosa María Payá, Cuban activist and human rights defender, has led initiatives such as the "Cuba Decide" campaign, which advocates for a referendum to allow Cubans to decide their country's political system. Payá, daughter of the late dissident Oswaldo Payá, has continued her father's legacy in the fight for democracy and freedom in Cuba. Rosa María Payá has been a crucial voice in promoting democracy and human rights in Cuba. Through his activism, he has raised the international profile of the Cuban cause, seeking international support and mobilizing the international community to advocate for free and fair elections in Cuba.

Influencers can potentially be agents of social change and promote social responsibility. They can mobilize their supporters by raising awareness, advocating, fundraising, and promoting behavior change, and they can positively impact society. The examples of Leonardo DiCaprio, Lizzo, Alexander Otaola, and Rosa María Payá demonstrate how influencers can lead successful social responsibility campaigns and contribute to important causes. Influencers can help create a more just and sustainable world by using their influence ethically and effectively.

Chapter 23: Leadership and Diversity

Diversity in leadership is essential to success and innovation in any organization. Including various perspectives, experiences, and backgrounds in leadership positions not only enriches decision-making but also reflects and respects the diversity of society at large. Below are key reasons why diversity is essential in leadership:

Diverse leadership teams tend to make more balanced and informed decisions. Diversity of perspectives allows leaders to consider broader solutions and better anticipate challenges and opportunities. By including people of different genders, ages, and ethnic and cultural backgrounds, leaders can avoid groupthink and consider multiple points of view before deciding.

Diversity fosters innovation and creativity. People with different backgrounds and experiences bring unique ideas and approaches, which can lead to novel and creative solutions. Diverse teams are more likely to question the status quo and think outside the box, which is crucial in a competitive and ever-changing business environment.

Organizations with diverse leadership can better understand and serve an equally diverse customer base. This is especially important in global markets, where products and services must be relevant to different cultures and preferences. Inclusive leadership can help organizations develop marketing strategies and products that resonate with many customers.

Organizations that promote diversity in leadership are often more attractive to talented employees who value inclusion and equity. Employees are more likely to feel valued and respected in an environment where diversity is celebrated. Additionally, representation in leadership can inspire employees from underrepresented groups to aspire to leadership roles, improving talent retention and development.

Diversity in leadership also strengthens an organization's reputation. Companies that promote diversity are seen as fairer and more ethical, which can improve their public image and enhance the trust of consumers, investors, and other stakeholders. Additionally, diverse organizations are often better positioned to address social responsibility and ethics issues, which can be a crucial differentiator in the marketplace.

Strategies to Promote Inclusive Leadership.

Establish Diversity and Inclusion Policies. Establishing apparent diversity and inclusion policies is one of the first strategies to foster inclusive leadership. These policies should outline the organization's commitment to equal opportunity and inclusion of all employees, regardless of gender, race, ethnicity, sexual orientation, age, disability, or other characteristics. Policies should also include goals and metrics to measure progress on diversity and inclusion.

Create an Inclusive Work Environment. Fostering inclusive leadership requires creating a work environment where all employees feel valued and respected. This includes promoting a culture of respect and fairness, eliminating bias and discrimination, and encouraging open and honest communication. Leaders must role model inclusive behavior and be committed to listening to and addressing employee concerns.

Offer Training and Development in Diversity and Inclusion. Training and continuous development are essential to foster inclusive leadership. Organizations should offer training programs addressing unconscious bias, intercultural communication, and diversity management. Mentoring and coaching programs can also help develop inclusive leadership skills and support the professional growth of employees from underrepresented groups.

Promote Diverse Representation in Leadership. Promoting diverse representation at leadership levels is crucial. This may involve identifying and removing barriers that prevent the advancement of underrepresented groups, such as biases in hiring and promotion processes. Organizations should set specific goals to increase diversity in leadership and take proactive steps to identify and develop diverse talent.

Facilitate Support Networks and Communities. Support networks and communities are valuable tools for fostering inclusion and diverse leadership. These networks can provide mentoring, resources, and emotional support to employees from underrepresented groups. Organizations can facilitate the creation of affinity groups and employee networks and support their participation in diversity events and conferences.

Evaluate and Improve Continuously. Continuous evaluation is critical to the success of diversity and inclusion initiatives. Organizations should collect data on employee representation and experience and use this data to identify areas for improvement. Work climate surveys and performance evaluations can provide valuable information about the effectiveness of inclusion policies and practices. Based on this data, organizations must adjust and improve their strategies to promote inclusive leadership.

Diversity in leadership is essential to the success and sustainability of organizations in the modern world. Benefits include better decision-making, incredible innovation and creativity, better connection with a diverse customer base, and significant talent attraction and retention. To foster inclusive leadership, organizations must establish clear policies, create an inclusive work environment, provide training and development, promote diverse representation, facilitate support networks, and continually evaluate their efforts. By doing so, they can create a culture of inclusion that respects and values diversity and drives organizational success and positive social impact.

Chapter 24: Influencers and Diversity

Social media are potent platforms where perceptions are shaped and messages are spread, making influencers critical in promoting diversity and inclusion. Representation and inclusion on social media refers to the visibility and fair representation of different groups and communities in digital content.

Influencers can use their platforms to highlight and represent various groups and communities, including different genders, races, ethnicities, sexual orientations, abilities, and cultures. In doing so, they contribute to a more fair and equitable representation of society. Diverse representation on social media is crucial because it helps normalize diversity and challenge negative or limiting stereotypes.

Influencers can use their platform to amplify the voices of individuals and groups traditionally marginalized or underrepresented in the media. This may include sharing the content of other minority content creators, collaborating with them, or highlighting their stories and experiences. Influencers help raise awareness about social injustices and promote inclusion by giving visibility to these voices.

Influencers can create content that celebrates diversity and promotes inclusion. This may include using inclusive language, promoting products and services from diverse brands, and creating content that addresses diversity, equity, and inclusion topics. Additionally, influencers can participate in campaigns that promote awareness of discrimination and foster a culture of respect and acceptance.

Influencers have the opportunity to challenge the stereotypes and prejudices that exist in society. They can use their platforms to challenge and dismantle preconceptions about different groups and to educate their followers about cultural, ethnic, and social diversity. In doing so, influencers can contribute to a more nuanced and empathetic understanding of differences.

Influencers can promote an inclusive environment among their followers, encouraging respect and acceptance of all people. This includes moderating comments to prevent hate speech and discrimination and encouraging constructive and respectful conversations about diversity and inclusion issues. By setting standards of inclusive behavior, influencers can create a more positive and welcoming online community.

Importance of Promoting Diversity.

Promoting diversity is crucial both on social media and in society in general for several reasons:

Reflection of Social Reality.

Diversity is a fundamental reality of global society. Promoting diversity on social media helps reflect this reality and shows the wealth of experiences and perspectives. Diverse representation in the media is essential for all groups to feel seen and valued.

Empowerment of Marginalized Communities.

Promoting diversity empowers marginalized communities by giving them a platform to express their voices and experiences. This not only increases their visibility but also provides them with an opportunity to influence the conversations and decisions that affect their lives.

Education and Awareness.

Influencers who promote diversity educate their followers about different cultures, stories, and social issues. This can help break down barriers and prejudices, fostering greater understanding and empathy between people from various backgrounds. Education about diversity is crucial to building a more just and equal society.

Innovation and creativity.

Diversity fosters innovation and creativity by bringing together various perspectives and approaches. This is true both in the content influencers create and the interactions they facilitate among their followers. A diverse community is a source of innovative ideas and solutions.

Construction of a Culture of Inclusion and Equity.

Promoting diversity is crucial in building a culture of inclusion and equity. This involves representing different groups and ensuring that everyone has the same opportunities to participate and be heard. Influencers can influence culture and social norms and can use this power to advocate for more significant equity and inclusion.

Diversity and inclusion on social media are essential to building a fair and equitable representation of society. Influencers play a crucial role in representing diverse groups, amplifying marginalized voices, creating inclusive content, challenging stereotypes, and fostering an inclusive environment among their followers. Promoting diversity reflects social reality and empowers marginalized communities, educates the public, encourages innovation, and helps build a culture of inclusion and equity. Influencers can contribute significantly to a more just and diverse society through these actions.

Chapter 25: Training Future Leaders

Training future leaders is crucial to ensure the success and sustainability of organizations and society in general. Programs and strategies designed to develop leadership skills must be inclusive, innovative, and adapted to the needs of new generations. Below are some of the key strategies and programs to develop future leaders:

Educational institutions play a fundamental role in training future leaders. Leadership programs can be integrated into school and university curricula, allowing students to develop leadership skills early. This includes fostering skills such as decision-making, effective communication, conflict resolution, and critical thinking.

Many organizations offer corporate leadership development programs to identify and cultivate internal talent, typically including formal training, workshops, hands-on experiences, and mentoring opportunities. Employees selected for these programs receive training in leadership skills, project management, and business strategies, preparing them to assume leadership roles within the organization.

Soft skills such as emotional intelligence, empathy, negotiation, and time management are essential for effective leadership. Training programs should include modules focusing on developing the skills necessary for team management, conflict resolution, and creating a positive work environment.

Practical experience is essential to the development of influential leaders. Organizations can offer opportunities for employees to take on leadership roles on specific projects, lead teams, or participate in strategic initiatives. This hands-on experience allows future leaders to apply what they have learned in a real-world setting and develop confidence in their abilities.

Mentoring and coaching are powerful tools for developing leaders. Mentoring programs pair less experienced employees with more experienced leaders who can offer guidance, support, and advice. Conversely, coaching can provide a more formal structure for developing specific skills and setting leadership goals.

Given the increasing focus on diversity and inclusion, leadership training programs must include modules on these topics. Future leaders must be equipped to manage diverse teams and promote an inclusive culture. Diversity and inclusion training helps leaders understand the importance of these issues and develop strategies to foster an equitable work environment.

The Importance of Mentoring and Education in Leadership.

Mentoring allows the transmission of knowledge and experiences from one generation of leaders to the next. Mentors can share the lessons they have learned and strategies and approaches to overcoming challenges. This knowledge transfer is invaluable to future leaders, providing them with a solid foundation on which to build their skills and strategies.

Mentoring and coaching offer personalized support and guidance tailored to each leader-in-training's specific needs and objectives. Mentors can help identify strengths and areas for improvement, set development goals, and provide constructive feedback. This personalized support is crucial for future leaders' professional and personal growth.

Mentoring also provides opportunities to develop professional networks and relationships. Mentors can introduce their mentees to other leaders, open doors to new opportunities, and help build a valuable network. These relationships can be critical to professional development and long-term success.

Mentors and educators act as role models for future leaders. Mentors can inspire their mentees to aspire to leadership roles and develop a strong work ethic through their behavior, values, and approach. Role modeling also helps trainees understand the expectations and responsibilities associated with leadership.

Leadership education focuses on acquiring technical knowledge and developing critical thinking and innovation. Educational programs can challenge future leaders to question the status quo, explore new ideas and approaches, and develop innovative solutions to complex problems. This is crucial in an ever-changing business and social environment.

Mentoring and education prepare future leaders for the challenges and opportunities of the future. As organizations and society evolve, leaders must have the skills, knowledge, and perspectives to navigate a dynamic environment and address emerging challenges. Continuing education and lifelong learning are essential to maintaining relevance and effectiveness in leadership roles.

Training future leaders is a crucial investment for the success and sustainability of organizations and society. Leadership development programs and strategies must be inclusive, innovative, and adapted to the needs of new generations. Mentoring and education play a critical role in this process, providing knowledge, support, inspiration, and opportunities for personal and professional growth. By focusing on the comprehensive development of hard and soft skills and fostering a culture of continuous learning, organizations can prepare leaders ready to meet future challenges and lead successfully in an ever-evolving world.

Chapter 26: Training of Influencers of the Future

Training the next generation of influencers is essential to ensure those who excel on social media can use their platform responsibly and effectively. As influencer marketing continues to grow, new content creators must be equipped with the skills and knowledge necessary to navigate a complex digital environment.

Any influencer must have a solid foundation in communication skills. This includes creating clear, engaging, and coherent content, both written and visual. Future influencers must be trained in storytelling, video editing, photography, and graphic design techniques to produce high-quality content that resonates with their audience. Additionally, they must understand how to optimize their content for different platforms and audiences.

Influencers must learn to develop and maintain a solid and authentic personal brand identity. This involves defining your values, mission, tone, and unique style. Consistency in personal branding is crucial to building trust with followers and establishing a recognizable presence in the market. Future influencers should know how their actions and content affect their brand and public perception.

Knowledge of how social media platforms' algorithms work and the ability to analyze performance data are critical skills for influencers. Interpreting statistics such as engagement, reach, and audience demographics allow influencers to adjust their content and strategy to maximize their impact. Training in data analysis and social media metrics is essential for making informed content creation and promotion decisions.

Future influencers must learn to manage relationships with brands, agencies, and other influencers. This includes skills in negotiation, professional communication, and project management. Establishing and maintaining strong business relationships is crucial to success in influencer marketing. Additionally, influencers must be trained to identify collaboration opportunities that align with their values and audience.

Future influencers must understand their rights and responsibilities regarding intellectual property and digital rights. This includes knowledge of copyright, trademark, and licensing laws. Education on these topics helps influencers protect their content and respect the work of others, avoiding legal and ethical problems.

Social responsibility and ethics must be pillars in influencer training. Future content creators must be aware of the impact of their messages and actions on their audience and society at large. This includes promoting responsible behavior, transparency in brand collaborations, and avoiding misleading or harmful content. Ethics training helps influencers make accountable and informed decisions in their work.

The Importance of Education and Ethics in Influencer Marketing.

Education in Ethics and Transparency.

Ethics education ensures influencers understand the importance of honesty and transparency in their relationships with audiences and brands. Influencers should know the need to disclose sponsored partnerships and paid content by advertising regulations and guidelines. Transparency is not only a legal obligation but also essential to maintain trust and credibility with followers.

Promotion of Responsible and Sensitive Content.

Ethics education also includes creating content that is responsible and sensitive to different audiences and cultures. Influencers must be informed about how their content may affect other groups and avoid stereotypes, prejudices, or discrimination. Diversity and inclusion training can help influencers be more aware and respectful in their communication.

Sustainable Use of Platforms and Resources.

Influencers must be educated on the sustainable use of digital platforms and resources. This includes understanding the environmental impact of content production and encouraging more sustainable practices, such as reducing digital waste and using clean energy platforms. It's crucial for influencers to align their activities with more responsible practices, as this can inspire their audience to do the same.

Training in Crisis Management and Social Responsibility.

Influencers must be prepared to handle crises and take responsibility for their actions. Crisis management training may include strategies for addressing criticism, public apologies, and responding effectively to adverse situations. Social responsibility also involves commitment to important causes and using the platform to promote positive change.

Promotion of Continuous Learning and Adaptability.

The digital environment constantly evolves, so influencers must commit to continuous learning and adaptability. This includes staying current with the latest trends, technologies, and policy changes on social media platforms. Training programs should foster a mindset of growth and adaptability, preparing future influencers to navigate a dynamic environment.

Training the next generation of influencers is essential to ensure new content creators use their platforms ethically and effectively. Through education in communication, personal branding, data analytics, relationship management, digital rights, and social responsibility, future influencers can develop the skills necessary to stand out and maintain integrity in their work. Ethics education is critical to ensure transparency, responsible content creation, and sustainability. By focusing on these aspects, training programs can prepare influencers to meet influencer marketing challenges and contribute positively to society and digital culture.

Chapter 27: False Leaders and Influencers: Clouds that Darken the World

In the vast and complex digital landscape, only some people who take on the role of leader or influencer do so with integrity or a positive purpose. False leaders and influencers use their platforms and visibility to spread misinformation, pursue personal interests, or manipulate followers for selfish gain. These individuals can act as "clouds" that obscure the world, creating confusion, division, and social harm.

Disinformation and Manipulation.

One of the most damaging characteristics of false leaders and influencers is their tendency to spread misinformation. This may include spreading conspiracy theories, fake news, or biased information that confuses and misleads their followers. These individuals can manipulate the truth to promote personal or political agendas, causing societal confusion and polarization.

Promotion of Harmful Content.

False leaders and influencers often promote content that is harmful to their followers' mental, physical, or emotional health. This may include glorifying dangerous behaviors, promoting unregulated or unethical products, or perpetuating harmful stereotypes. This type of content is not only irresponsible, but it can also have real negative consequences for the people who consume it.

Exploitation of Followers.

Many false leaders and influencers seek to exploit their followers for financial or other gain. This may include selling fraudulent products, promoting get-rich-quick schemes, or exploiting fan loyalty for economic or political support. Exploitation can be particularly insidious when masked under the guise of a noble cause or community support.

Lack of Transparency and Authenticity.

A key characteristic of false leaders and influencers is a lack of transparency and authenticity. These individuals may hide their true intentions, connections, or financial compensations behind their online activities. This lack of honesty undermines trust and credibility, leading followers to make decisions based on incomplete or misleading information.

Creation of Toxic Environments.

False leaders and influencers can foster toxic environments online, where hate, discrimination, and polarization prevail. These individuals can create a culture of confrontation and negativity by stoking tensions and divisions. This is especially concerning when online words and actions can translate into real-world consequences off-screen.

Impact of False Leaders and Influencers on Society.

Erosion of Public Trust.

Plenty of false leaders and influencers can erode public trust in institutions, media, and authority figures. When these individuals are discovered to have misled their followers, faith in the honesty and integrity of the information available is undermined. This loss of trust can have long-term consequences for social cohesion and society's ability to address collective problems.

Spread of Disinformation.

Disinformation spread by false leaders and influencers can seriously affect public health, security, and social cohesion. For example, spreading vaccine conspiracy theories can lead to declining vaccination, increasing the risk of disease outbreaks. Likewise, promoting fake or biased news can fuel political polarization and social division.

Normalization of Negative Behaviors.

False leaders and influencers can contribute to the normalization of irresponsible or unethical behavior in society by promoting it. This may include promoting cancel culture, online harassment, or economic exploitation. When these behaviors become normalized, it is more difficult for society to establish and maintain ethical and moral standards.

Damage to Mental and Emotional Health.

Harmful content promoted by false leaders and influencers can hurt the mental and emotional health of followers. This includes perpetuating unrealistic beauty standards, glorifying unhealthy lifestyles, or promoting negative attitudes toward certain groups. These messages can contribute to problems such as low self-esteem, anxiety, and depression.

Obstacles to Positive Change.

Finally, false leaders and influencers can act as obstacles to positive change. By diverting attention and resources from legitimate causes or promoting divisive agendas, they can make it challenging to mobilize collective efforts to address significant social problems. This can slow progress in critical areas such as social justice, equality, and sustainability.

False leaders and influencers represent a significant challenge to contemporary society. Their ability to spread misinformation, exploit their followers, and promote harmful behavior can have severe and long-lasting consequences. Followers must develop critical thinking skills and can discern between genuine and deceptive influences. Additionally, social media platforms, media outlets, and regulators have a crucial role in mitigating the impact of these individuals, promoting transparency and accountability. By working together, we can lift the "clouds" of misinformation and manipulation and move toward a more informed, fair, and ethical world.

Chapter 28: Fusion between Leader and Influencer: Let's Overcome the Shadows

In the contemporary world, the distinction between traditional leaders and influencers is blurring, giving rise to a hybrid figure that combines the qualities of both roles. Both leaders and influencers can influence the opinions, behaviors, and decisions of others, but they do so in different contexts and with various tools. Fusing these roles can be especially powerful in creating a positive and meaningful impact. Below explores how leaders and influencers can combine their strengths to "overcome the shadows" and meet contemporary challenges:

Communication is a crucial skill for both leaders and influencers. Traditional leaders, such as CEOs, politicians, or activists, often communicate strategic visions and organizational decisions, while influencers use social media to connect more personally and emotionally with their followers. Fusing these styles can result in more effective and authentic communication, inspiring and mobilizing a diverse audience.

Leaders are often visionaries who define the direction of organizations or movements, while influencers can quickly mobilize large audiences around specific causes. By combining these skills, leaders can leverage digital platforms and social influence to advance long-term visions and mobilize support for important initiatives. This is especially relevant in crisis or social change contexts, where clear leadership and effective mobilization are necessary.

Leaders influence through their example, acting as role models regarding ethics, values, and behavior. Influencers, for their part, significantly impact cultural norms and consumer behaviors. When a leader also acts as an influencer, they can promote positive values and ethical practices in a broad and accessible way, helping to establish cultural norms that reinforce social responsibility, sustainability, and inclusion.

The fusion of leadership and influence means greater accountability and transparency. Leaders and influencers must be transparent in their intentions, actions, and relationships with brands or organizations. This is crucial to maintaining public trust and ensuring that their influence is used ethically. Transparency also means being open about challenges and mistakes, which can humanize the leader and strengthen the connection with the audience.

Influencers are known for their ability to adapt quickly to new trends and technologies, while leaders are often responsible for guiding innovation within their organizations or communities. The combination of these qualities can result in leaders who are not only innovative but also agile and able to adapt quickly to a changing environment. This is essential in a world where technologies and social expectations constantly evolve.

Let's Overcome the Shadows: Using Positive Influence for Change...

"Overcoming the shadows" refers to overcoming challenges and obstacles that obscure clarity, justice, and progress. In the context of the fusion between leaders and influencers, this concept takes on a special meaning. Influencer-leaders can use their combined influence to address contemporary issues and foster positive societal change. Below are some key areas where this merger could be particularly impactful:

Promotion of Social Justice and Inclusion.

Leaders and influencers can use their platforms to advocate for social justice and inclusion, highlighting issues such as discrimination, inequality, and lack of representation. By elevating the voices of marginalized communities and promoting equal opportunity, they can help "overcome the shadows" of injustice and build a more equitable society.

Promotion of Environmental Sustainability.

Sustainability is a critical area where combined influence can make a significant difference. Influencers can promote sustainable practices, educate their audiences about climate change, and advocate for responsible environmental policies. By inspiring their followers to adopt more sustainable lifestyles, they can contribute to protecting the environment and fighting climate change.

Promotion of Health and Wellbeing.

Health and well-being are fundamental aspects of a prosperous society. Leaders and influencers can use their platform to promote mental health, physical well-being, and self-care. By destigmatizing mental health issues and encouraging healthy habits, they can help "beat the shadows" of health stigma and neglect.

Promotion of Education and Personal Development.

Education is a powerful tool for empowerment and social change. Leaders and influencers can promote the importance of continuing education and personal development, providing resources and motivation for learning and growth. Inspiring their followers to invest in their education and skills can help them "overcome the shadows" of ignorance and lack of opportunity.

Creating Resilient Communities.

In times of crisis, such as pandemics, natural disasters, or social conflicts, the ability to mobilize and support communities is crucial. Leaders and influencers can use their platform to coordinate relief efforts, provide accurate information, and promote community resilience. By unifying people around a common purpose, they can help "conquer the shadows" of fear and hopelessness.

The fusion between leaders and influencers represents a powerful convergence of skills and capabilities that can be used to address complex challenges and foster positive change. By combining vision and leadership with social influence and mobilization, leaders-influencers can inspire and guide their followers to "conquer the shadows" of injustice, inequity, climate change, and other critical issues. This new leadership figure can be crucial in building a more just, sustainable, and healthy future for all through effective communication, authenticity, transparency, and commitment to positive values.

Chapter 29: Conclusions and Reflections

Throughout this book, we have explored in depth the impact and responsibilities that accompany the roles of leaders and influencers in modern society. The convergence of leadership and influence is an increasingly evident phenomenon in an interconnected and digitalized world, where the ability to communicate and mobilize large audiences is crucial to addressing contemporary challenges.

Although operating in different contexts, traditional leaders and digital influencers share the ability to shape perceptions, influence behaviors, and guide people toward collective actions. Throughout the chapters, we have highlighted how leaders use their strategic vision and their ability to inspire to lead organizations, movements, or countries. In contrast, influencers use digital platforms to connect more personally and emotionally with their followers.

Our analysis's recurring theme is the importance of integrity and transparency. In an era of abundant information and often misinformation, authenticity is critical to establishing and maintaining public trust. Both leaders and influencers must be honest and transparent about their intentions, decisions, and partnerships. Transparency reinforces credibility and sets an ethical standard that others can follow.

Additionally, we have discussed the essential role of ethics and social responsibility. Leaders and influencers have a robust platform that can be used for the common good. Promoting positive values such as justice, equality, sustainability, and inclusion is an inherent responsibility of these roles. A genuine commitment to social and environmental well-being must accompany the ability to influence people's behavior. We have seen how promoting diversity and inclusion can enrich decision-making, foster innovation, and reflect the reality of a globally diverse society.

Adaptability and continuous learning emerge as critical competencies in an ever-changing global environment. Leaders and influencers must be prepared to face new challenges and opportunities, adapt to changing circumstances, and constantly seek new ways to grow and improve. This commitment to learning is essential to staying relevant and practical, especially in a rapidly evolving world of technologies and social dynamics.

A crucial aspect discussed has been the emergence of false leaders and influencers who use their platforms to spread misinformation and manipulate and exploit their followers. These individuals represent a significant threat to social cohesion and public trust. Its ability to create confusion and division underscores the need for critical discernment by the public and stricter regulation by platforms and authorities.

Finally, the fusion of leadership and influence is presented as a powerful combination that can be used to "overcome the shadows" that darken our world. Leaders and influencers have the unique ability to integrate strategic vision and social mobilization, addressing global problems such as climate change, inequality, and misinformation. By doing so, they can inspire and guide their followers towards positive and sustainable change.

In conclusion, leadership and influence are transformative forces in our society. Those who take on these roles must do so with a deep sense of responsibility, aware of their impact on the world. A commitment to ethics, transparency, and social justice must accompany the ability to lead and influence. By using their platform to promote the common good and address the most pressing challenges of our time, leaders and influencers can contribute to building a more just, equitable, and sustainable future for all. This book has sought to provide guidance and reflection on how we can move towards that future, using the power of leadership and influence consciously and positively.